Using Age Progression

Understanding Life's Journey

Joyce Hopewell

HopeWell
Knutsford, England

First published in the U.K. in 2013 by HopeWell

HopeWell
130 Grove Park, Knutsford
Cheshire WA16 8QD, U.K.

Copyright © Joyce Hopewell 2013

All rights reserved. No part of this publication may be reproduced, sorted in a retrieval system, or transmitted in any form or by any means, electronic or otherwise, without the prior permission of the publisher. Reviewers may quote brief passages.

Edited by Barry Hopewell

ISBN 978-0-9558339-6-0

Dedicated to

Bruno & Louise Huber, who researched and developed the theory of the Life Clock and Age Progression

Acknowledgements

I would like to thank those people who have co-operated in my research, giving freely of their time, and who have agreed to let me use their charts and experiences as examples in this book: Allister, Grace, Sarah, Sally, Philip, Laura, Michael, Sybille, Gareth, Bee, Roger, Phoebe, Paula, Lorna, Sue, Margaret, Denise, Kitty, David, Suzy and Imogen.

I would also like to thank the Astrological Association of Great Britain (www.astrologicalassociation.com) for their permission to include material from articles that I wrote which have appeared in the Astrological Journal on Berthe Morisot, Fred Astaire, Henri Cartier-Bresson, Meryl Streep and Alan Turing.

Contents

Foreword	vii
Introduction and Overview of Age Progression	1
The Huber-style Chart and the Five Levels	3
The Life Clock and Age Progression	6
Part 1	
Age Progression and the Houses	11
The 1st Quadrant: 1st, 2nd and 3rd houses	12
Allister: 1st House Stellium	13
Grace: Empty First House	14
The 2nd Quadrant: 4th, 5th and 6th houses	16
Prince William: 5th House Venus	17
Sarah: 6th House Focus	18
The 3rd Quadrant: 7th, 8th and 9th Houses	19
Fred Astaire: 7th House Neptune	20
The 4th Quadrant: 10th, 11th and 12th Houses	22
Pablo Picasso: 10th House Focus	24
Part 2	
House Zones, Balance Point and Low Point	25
Cardinal, Fixed and Mutable Zones	26
Charles Dickens: Age Point in Cardinal Zone	27
The Balance Point	28
Sally: Age Point on Balance Point	28
The Low Point	29
Mid-Life Crisis	30
Philip: Age Point on Low Point	31
The Stress Area	33
Psychological View of Houses	33
Laura: Empty 'You' Side	34
Part 3	
Age Progression and the Signs	36
Age Point changing from Fire to Earth	38
Michael: Fire to Earth	39
Age Point changing from Earth to Air	40
Sybille: Earth to Air	40
Age Point changing from Air to Water	42
Author's Chart: Air to Water	42
Age Point changing from Water to Fire	43
Gareth: Water to Fire	43

Part 4
Age Progression and Aspects to Planets   45
  Timing and Intensity   46
  Age Point in Conjunction   47
    Charles Dickens: Age Point Conjunct Mercury   *48*
    Bee: Age Point conjunct Jupiter   *50*
    Margaret Thatcher: Age Point conjunct Moon/Neptune   *52*
  Age Point in Opposition   53
    Emile Zola: Age Point opposite Sun   *54*
    Roger: Age Point opposite Jupiter   *56*
  Age Point in Semi-sextile Aspect   57
  Age Point in Sextile Aspect   57
  Age Point in Square Aspect   58
    Phoebe: Age Point square Sun/Mercury   *59*
    Author's Chart: Age Point square Uranus   *61*
  Age Point in Trine Aspect   63
  Age Point in Quincunx Aspect   63
    Paula: Age Point quincunx Pluto   *64*
    Lorna: Age Point quincunx Pluto   *65*
    Margaret: Age Point quincunx Pluto   *66*
  Transits and the Age Point   68
    Sue: Intense combined Transit and Age Point experience   *68*

Part 5
Age Progression in the Moon Node Chart   70
  Psychological meaning of the Moon Node Chart   70
    Author's Moon Node and Natal Charts   *71*
  Age Progression in the Moon Node Chart   72

Part 6
Chart Interpretations – Age Progression at Work   73
    Berthe Morisot: A Woman in a Man's World   *74*
    Fred Astaire: "Can't act. Slightly bald. Also dances."   *80*
    Denise: Seeker and Teacher   *86*
    Henri Cartier-Bresson: Image Maker   *91*
    Kitty: Practicality in Action   *97*
    Meryl Streep: A Class Act   *102*
    David: The Warp and Weft of Life   *108*
    Suzanne Fischer: A Passion for Music   *114*
    Alan Turing: Father of Computer Science   *119*
    Imogen: A Healing Touch   *125*

Part 7
Summary and Conclusion   131
  What to consider when using Age Progression   131
  Conclusion   137

Resources   139

Foreword

Imagine that everything in the world is interconnected, in ways that science does not really understand. Quantum theory, morphic resonance and other scientific theories give a hint; modern psychologies developed from Carl Jung's collective unconscious and synchronicity give further hints, as do modern psycho/spiritual evolutionary theories such as those reflected in Ken Wilber's Integral world view.

Imagine that there is a system that can give some idea of the patterns within this interconnected whole, and can relate the individual being to the state of the whole. There is indeed such a system that has existed and evolved for millennia; it is roughly characterised by the term 'astrology'.

Imagine further that the life of an individual in space-time and the individual life story themselves are in some way reflected in the state of the whole at the beginning of that life, and that reflection includes the potentially most significant psycho-spiritual occurrences in that life story. There are indeed such 'timing' systems within astrology; perhaps the most sophisticated being Age Progression through the Life Clock developed after extensive research by Swiss astrologer/psychologists Bruno & Louise Huber.

You can use Age Progression to seek meaning in the jumble of events in your life. It can show what sort of influences are likely to be at work at different stages of this particular lifetime. As you give meaning to particular times of your life, you tell stories of how things are and how they might be. Naturally this helps in navigating your way forwards through life.

Of course, you can use Age Progression in consultation with a friend or client. Many practitioners regard it as a 'gilt edged' technique saving many hours of counselling.

In this book, Joyce Hopewell explores the different facets of Age Progression, illuminated by extensive examples, to help you to understand how to apply it to yourself and to helping others.

You will be well rewarded by any efforts you make to apply this 'gilt-edged' technique!

Barry Hopewell
Editor

Introduction and Overview of Age Progression

Of the many techniques used in the Huber Method of astrological psychology, Age Progression – using the natal chart as a life clock – is more often than not the technique which captures the imagination and interest of newcomers and seasoned astrologers alike. You might wonder why this would be so, but stop for a moment and consider this question. If you had a tool which identified precisely where you are now in your life journey, and which took into account the psychological and developmental phase you're currently moving through, together with what this means for you as a unique individual, wouldn't you want to use it?

Drawing on the energy dynamic of the houses, not the zodiac signs, Age Progression and the Age Point can be used to trace the developmental and psychological phases of life from birth through childhood and adolescence and on into maturity. Using specific techniques it is possible to chart the life journey and significant life experiences of any individual. Age Progression and the movement of the Age Point can be used for personal development and greater self-understanding when working on your own chart, and as it is not static, it can be a very useful resource if we hit a rough patch in life. It offers insights into what is being experienced, and how, as well as showing that things will move on; we do not need to be stuck there indefinitely, unless we choose to. With study and experience, Age Progression can be used effectively as a personal tool, and it can be used with clients by professional astrologers and counsellors trained in astrological psychology.

This unique approach to timing in the horoscope differs from other more traditional and conventional methods which concentrate on cyclic planetary movements and their transits to the planets in the natal chart. The beauty and attraction of Age Progression lies in its simplicity. It is a clear and straightforward technique to use, and it yields very valuable and rewarding results. But bear in mind that for Age Progression to work effectively, **an accurate time of birth is essential**.

2 *Using Age Progression*

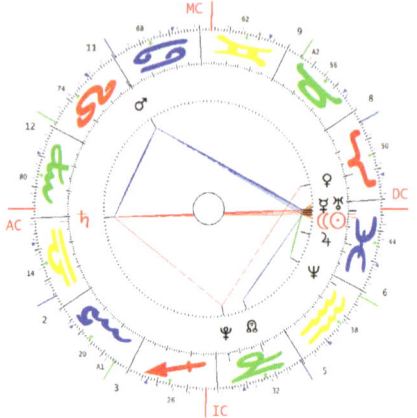

A Huber-Style Chart

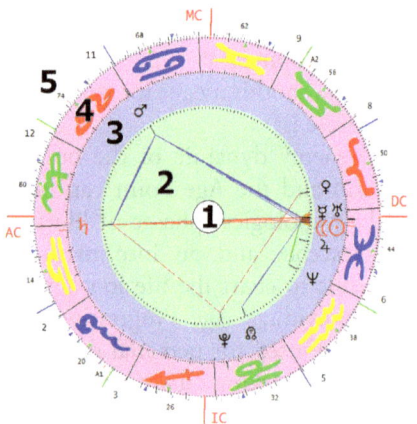

Shading to Illustrate the Five Levels

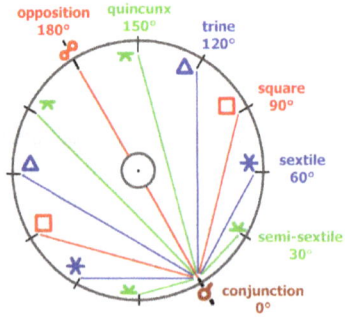

Ptolemaic Arrangement of the Aspects

Before getting into Age Progression, there are certain things that you need to understand, particularly if you have not previously studied astrological psychology[*1].

The Huber-style Chart and the Five Levels

Bruno Huber was a pioneer in the use of colour in the chart, based on his understanding of the psychology of colour. You can see an example chart opposite.

In astrological psychology the birth chart is interpreted in five distinct and independent levels, illustrated in the shaded chart below the example. These are the five levels:

1. The **centre circle** symbolises the inner, higher self, the central core of the person.
2. The **aspect pattern** represents inner unconscious motivation.
3. The **planets** represent our psychological drives.
4. The **signs** of the zodiac represent inherited traits and qualities.
5. The **houses** represent the environment around us, the outside world.

The basic rule is: Do not mix up the levels. Interpretive features at one level should not be mixed up with those at another level – for example, aspects are not drawn between planets and the angles (AC, DC, MC, IC) as the angles are on the level of the houses, which is separate from the level of the planets.

The Centre Circle

The circle at the centre of the chart represents our essential inner self, the unknown source of our life, identity, will and consciousness. From here, energy flows out through the aspect pattern and the planets, coloured by the signs, into the world of the houses. All interpretative work begins with this circle in the centre, which acknowledges not only the unique inner being of each individual, but also the connection with spirit, soul and universal energy.

The Aspect Pattern

The only aspects used in astrological psychology are those of 30 degrees, illustrated in the Ptolemaic Arrangement (opposite). The aspects are coloured according to their essential quality: **cardinal = red**, **fixed = blue**, **mutable = green**. The colour **orange** is used for conjunctions.

Meaning of the Aspect Pattern

"This is where we look to see the unconscious driving forces of the individual. The aspects are pulsating with energy of different kinds and qualities, and the aspect structure offers valuable information about what makes us "tick", what really drives us.

The motivation shown here is largely unconscious, but we can get to know and understand it better – and we can choose to work on familiarizing ourselves with what truly makes us "tick". Anything that is unconscious, such as our inner motivation, can be brought into consciousness. We can recognise it, we can accept it and we can begin to work with it. Then we can start to transform it, change it, integrate it, and allow it to become an integrated part of our lives. Such integration and development of the 'whole' person is the aim of the approach to psychology known as psychosynthesis.

Although the motivation shown in this part of the chart might start off by being unconscious, we can thus bring it into greater awareness so that we can move forward feeling more firmly in the driving seat of our lives."

quoted from The Cosmic Egg Timer[*1]

We can learn a lot about motivation from the perceived image, colour, shaping and direction of the aspect pattern and the individual aspect figures found therein. See e.g. *The Cosmic Egg Timer*[*1].

The Planets

Astrological psychology uses just the seven classical planets, the three outer (transpersonal) planets (including Pluto) and the Moon's North Node. In charts, the three personality or ego planets Sun (will/mind), Moon (feelings) and Saturn (body) are normally drawn in red. See table of planets and their glyphs.

Ego Planets		**Tool Planets**		**Transpersonal Planets**	
Sun	☉	Mercury	☿	Uranus	♅
Moon	☽	Venus	♀	Neptune	♆
Saturn	♄	Mars	♂	Pluto	♇
		Jupiter	♃		

ascending Moon Node ☊

The Planets and their Glyphs

Aspect Orbs

The psychological researches of the Hubers established the figures in the table below to give orbs appropriate for astrological psychology and thus, in particular, for interpretation of aspects from the Age Point.

Planet	⚹	⚻ ✶	□	△	☌ ☍
☉ ☽	3°	5°	6°	8°	9°
☿ ♀ ♃	2°	4°	5°	6°	7°
♂ ♄	1½°	3°	4°	5°	6°
♅ ♆ ♇	1°	2°	3°	4°	5°

Aspect Orbs

The Signs of the Zodiac

The signs represent inherited traits and characteristics and influence the energy of planets contained within them. They are coloured according to their element: **fire = red**, **earth = green**, **air = yellow**, **water = blue**.

Aries	♈	♎	Libra
Taurus	♉	♏	Scorpio
Gemini	♊	♐	Sagittarius
Cancer	♋	♑	Capricorn
Leo	♌	♒	Aquarius
Virgo	♍	♓	Pisces

The Signs of the Zodiac

The Houses

The twelve houses represent our environment – the influence of family, friends, social contacts and so on. We use standard abbreviations for the angles of the chart i.e. Ascendant (AC), Descendant (DC), Imum Coeli (IC) and Medium Coeli (MC). The two hemispheres and four quadrants bounded by them have specific psychological meanings.

Koch House System

The Koch house system is used because it allows for precise psychological analysis, and because it is based on time. This is not because of some whim or random choice, but because Bruno Huber extensively researched various house systems using Age Progression and found that the Koch system gave the most reliable and consistent results.

I have been using the Huber Method, and this particular technique, since 1986, and I still find it quite awesome in its accuracy when working with clients. Age Progression allows me to home in on what might be happening in the life of my client, both psychologically and in the context of ongoing events and experiences. It allows me to get alongside them in the place where they are now, because I have a better understanding of where they are coming from, and what psychological life phase they are going through. Age Progression also offers many insights into the nature of the person's earlier life experiences so that I – and any other astrologer using the Huber Method of astrological psychology – am able to view the client's life journey as a more rounded and fleshed out, three-dimensional whole. As the Koch system has houses of unequal size, this is another factor which is taken into consideration when working with Age Progression.

The Life Clock and Age Progression

The concept of using the chart as a Life Clock[*2] is simple. The hand of the life clock – the Age Point – starts moving when we are born, at the Ascendant (AC). It moves in an anti-clockwise direction around the chart, taking six years to travel through each house, regardless of the size of the house. At age 18 it reaches the Immum Coeli or lower Midheaven (IC); at 36 it reaches the Descendant (DC). At 54 it is on the Midheaven (MC) and at age 72 it reaches the AC once again, ready to begin another circuit of the chart, but this time with a wealth of life experience to draw upon. As many more people are now living well beyond "three score years and ten" this second circuit of the chart can be highly significant in view of an ageing but still physically active population, many of whom are continuing to work way beyond the historically conventional age of retirement.

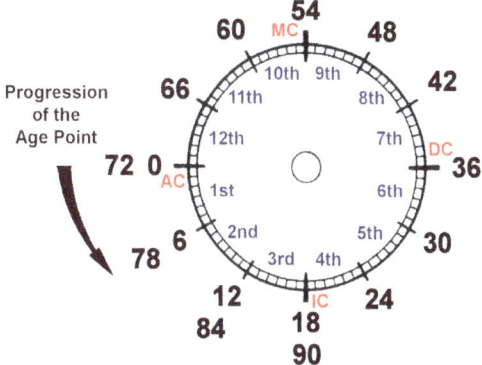

The Age Point moves around the Twelve Houses

The Dynamic Energy Curve

A fluid energy dynamic is present in each of the twelve houses of the chart[*3]. A surge of energy, coming from the central core of the chart, thrusts its way out to meet the surrounding environment. It peaks at each of the four cardinal points – the AC, DC, IC and MC – as it moves outwards into the world. These four cuspal points are all high energy areas in the context of Age Progression.

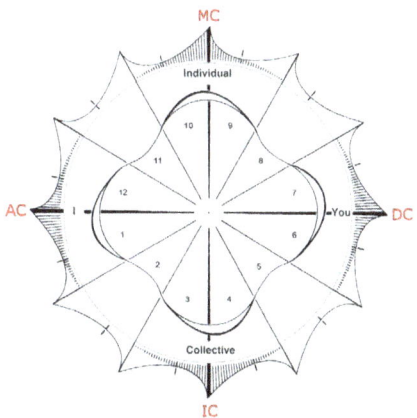

The Dynamic Energy Curve

This outward thrust is reflected by a corresponding smaller surge of energy around each of the house cusps. The energy peaks at the cusps, but then levels out at approximately one third of the way through the house[*4]. This is where we find the Balance Point. Here, the amount of

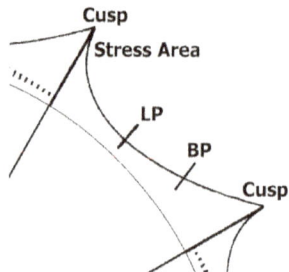

Balance Point and Low Point

energy available coming from within is roughly equal to the energy demands made upon the individual by the outside environment, meaning that when the Age Point reaches this place in each of the houses, we should be able to cope with life's demands relatively easily, and with a certain amount of poise and equilibrium.

The output of energy coming from the central core falls off after this, and is at its lowest ebb at the Low Point, which is found approximately two-thirds of the way through each house[*4]. At the Low Point there is a challenge; planets here can't easily be expressed in the environment and the individual is likely to find it hard to muster the energy and drive to participate so fully in the affairs of the house and the corresponding area of life where the Low Point is. Life may be a hard-going slog for a while as the focus and attention of energy at the Low Point is inward, making the person less responsive to the demands of the outside world, and less able to cope comfortably with them. A period of introspection and inner reflection is also likely to be happening for the individual at this time.

Life Phases

Age Progression covers 36 psychological life phases in the chart, each one relating to different life experiences spanning childhood to maturity. These are explored in this book. If you are working with the chart of another person, these life phases can help in understanding where that person are coming from in their life at the time of your meeting. This enables the astrological psychologist or counsellor to get alongside their client and empathise with their world view. Likewise, when using Age Progression for yourself, an understanding of these life phases can offer insights into your own experiences.

When using the Age Point we need to consider not only the house and psychological life phase which the Age Point is travelling through, but also the qualities of both the sign and its element. The zodiac signs and their associated elements form a backdrop to the ongoing activity and experiences within each house. Changes of sign can be significant events in the life journey as a complete change of energy is involved.

Aspects in Age Progression
It is important to bear in mind that Age Progression is concerned primarily with experiences and not events, although the two often go together. Age Progression highlights the psychological effect of life events on the individual, rather than focussing on the events themselves.

Aspects to planets made by the Age Point are a major factor to consider. The conjunction and opposition are strongest and tend to have the greatest and most immediate impact. Squares and quincunxes can also be powerful. The square tends to be challenging and can demand action; the quincunx can bring significant lessons about life and deep learning. The energy and quality of the planet involved will dominate and colour the experience. As it travels around the chart, the Age Point will also pick up and activate the aspect patterns present in the chart. This will offer opportunities to express the motivations, behaviour patterns and responses to life the aspect patterns indicate, along with any innate talents and skills they signify. Although we do not primarily work with transits using the Huber Method, it should be noted that if the Age Point is making an aspect to a planet when a transit to the same planet is taking place, a "double whammy" effect may be experienced, and this can be very powerful.

When the Age Point is half way between two planets, the midpoint position can also be significant. After the Age Point has made a conjunction to a planet, the orientation of the individual will be influenced for some time afterwards by that planet. As the Age Point moves away and continues its journey around the chart, it reaches the midpoint between the two planets. The focus and influence of the planet up ahead will then take over. This turning point can be important as the person will develop a new orientation in life, coloured by the qualities of the upcoming planet.

There are deeper and more detailed descriptions in this book of each of the features of Age Progression which have been outlined in this introduction, along with illustrations and examples. They are taken from real life and from the charts of well-known people, and it is hoped that they will inspire you, the reader, to work on your own chart in order to understand and appreciate what a powerful technique Age Progression is. Bruno Huber often encouraged students of astrological psychology to not just accept what was being taught and put forward in the seminars and books by himself and Louise Huber, but to test it out for themselves to see if it had significance for them. As a student of astrological psychology in the 1980s, I was very sceptical about Age Progression when I first encountered it and set out to "prove" it for myself using my own chart and the techniques you will read about in this book. I didn't really believe Age Progression could work and spent a considerable amount of time plotting psychologically significant times and events in my own life journey and correlating them with the Age Point in my chart. I was humbled and amazed at how accurate Age Progression turned out to be. And that was not just for me because I've used Age Progression with confidence ever since with my clients and students alike and have never once been disappointed.

As a student, I was told by my tutor that Age Progression was "gilt edged". Quite simply, it is!

Notes to Introduction

*1 For an introduction to astrological psychology, see *The Cosmic Egg Timer* by Joyce Hopewell and Richard Llewellyn.

*2 For an extensive and detailed description of Age Progression, see *LifeClock* by Bruno & Louise Huber.

*3 The energy dynamic in the houses and the use of Koch houses were first introduced in *The Astrological Houses* by Bruno & Louise Huber.

*4 The Balance Point and Low Point are usually marked on Huber-style charts (small blue and green triangles on the charts in this book); their distance from the cusp is actually in the proportion of the *Golden Ratio* or *Golden Mean*, rather than precisely one third. See e.g. *The Astrological Houses*.

Part 1

Age Progression and the Houses

The movement of the Age Point around the houses is a movement of time. It reflects the developmental psychological phases of life, beginning with birth, when the Age Point is conjunct the AC. Each of the houses in the chart has an overall psychological theme, and with twelve houses there are twelve different themes which correspond to different life phases. The chart can be divided into four Quadrants; each set of three houses relates to a different Quadrant, with its own element, quality and theme.

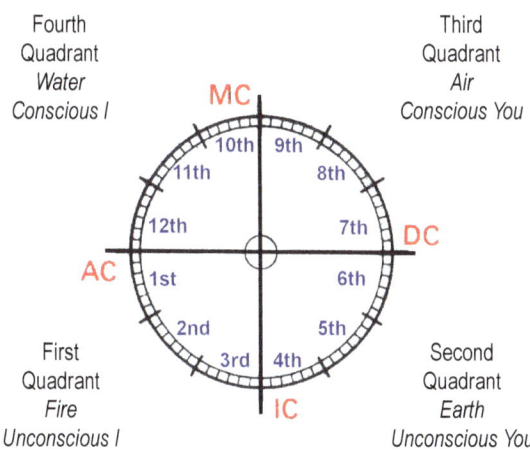

The Four Quadrants

The 1st Quadrant: 1st, 2nd and 3rd houses

This Quadrant spans the AC to the IC, covering the movement of the Age Point from birth to 18 years. It is associated with the element of Fire, and with impulsive actions. It's the realm of the Unconscious "I" and its main theme is self-assertion and survival.

The 1st house – Birth to 6 years
Formation of the "I"

Birth is one of the most traumatic experiences we undergo. As we are literally pushed out into the world, the environment we've gestated within for 9 months changes for ever. During the first 6 years of life we gradually develop a sense of ourselves as separate from our mother. To begin with we are in a symbiotic relationship with her but as we develop a sense of our own separateness and of ourselves as an individual "I" we go through a stage of obstinate defiance as this "I" – our sense of self – is established. This is the time of the "Terrible Twos" when toddlers learn to say "No" to almost everything and insist on doing things their way. The accompanying tantrums are often a result of the child needing to assert its individuality but not having the language skills to verbalise this, or their needs, hence the tantrum. The child is developing fast on all fronts, but still relies heavily on the environment for support and care. As the Age Point moves through this house, the child's sense of self as a separate "I" begins to stabilise as he or she interacts with and learns from experiences in the surrounding environment.

In the natal chart the 1st house is all about "Me" – "my" place where "I" am, where "I" reside and come from, and sometimes retreat to as well. If there are planets in the 1st house they will colour and shape the perception we have of ourselves and how we express this. If this house is empty, it doesn't mean that we have no sense of self, but rather that asserting and developing this is not such a strong focus of attention or a priority for us. The developmental psychological phase associated with this house will take place regardless of whether there are planets there or not. Let's take a look at the 1st house in a couple of charts.

Allister: 1st House Stellium

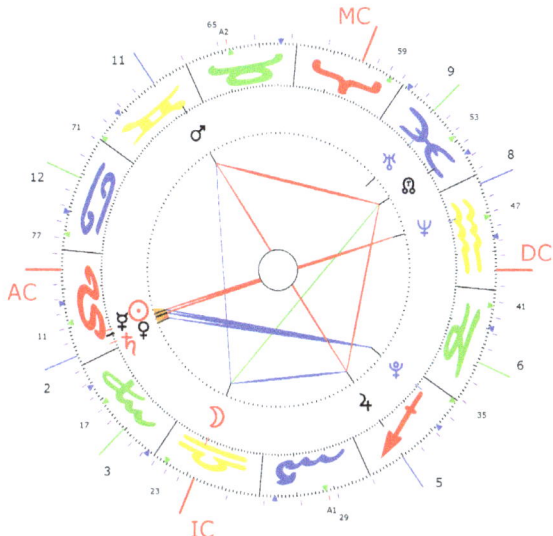

17.08.2007, 04:06, Bedford, England

Allister is a bright and lively child who demands attention and likes to be noticed. He is 5 years old and his 1st house is strongly emphasised by its stellium of Sun, Saturn, Mercury and Venus. All are in the flamboyant and fiery sign of Leo, and are in a stressed position[*5] just before the 2nd cusp. People with planets in such a position will constantly be expressing the energy of the stressed planets. Allister's Age Point will be conjunct all these planets between the ages of 5 and 6, at the very time when the stabilisation of the "I" is reaching completion. Allister, already in the process of forming a strong sense of himself, will be moving into what child psychologist Jean Piaget[*6] calls the stage of concrete operations – the beginning of a deeper understanding and mastery of his environment. He will use the planets there to help him in this task, asking questions, exploring his world in greater depth, discovering how things work and consolidating the knowledge and experience he is rapidly accumulating.

14   Using Age Progression

Grace: Empty First House

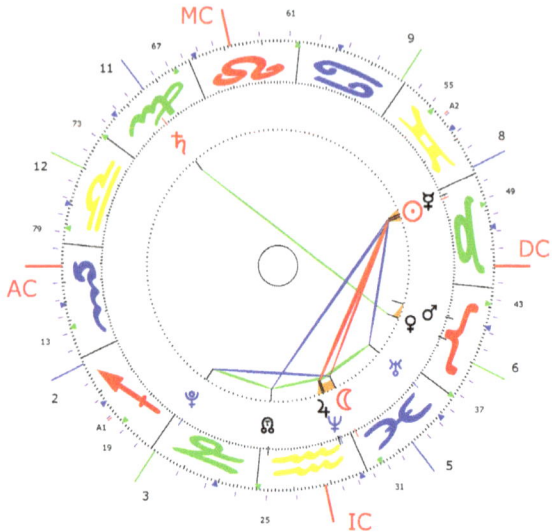

17.05.2009, 18:42, London, England

Grace has no planets in the 1st house. At the age of 3 she is at what Piaget calls the stage of intuitive thought, learning about her world through imaginative play, asking questions, listening to stories and conversations, picking up new words and phrases to try out, exploring and experimenting with the world around her. Grace's early years have been very challenging on a physical level as she was born with a genetic condition which meant she had to undergo several major operations in the first two years of life. Her main challenge has been to survive, and the psychological drive of the houses in the first Quadrant of the chart is survival.

The sign which occupies an empty house can often give significant insights into what might be going on in the individual's life. Grace has the sign of Scorpio in her 1st house, a sign associated with intensity, life and death, transformation and change. In the first two years of her life she spent several months in and out of hospital, undergoing the surgery which has enabled her now, as a 3 year old, to live a normal and relatively trouble-free life. In order to reach this stage, her physical being underwent a transformation, via the surgery, to alleviate and correct a condition which would have proved difficult to manage as she grew older. It was a time of extreme emotional stress for her parents, and a period of pain and discomfort for Grace. She hung on with tenacity and strength – reflecting the qualities of the sign her Age Point was travelling through – and is now making up for lost time as her development moves forward in leaps and bounds.

The 2nd house – 6 to 12 years
Creation of personal life and awareness of possessions

The 2nd house focuses on possessions and the growing child moving through this stage develops a taste for collecting objects and treasures. You may remember, as a child, having a treasure box where special things you collected and found interesting were kept. These would have been taken out from time to time to look at, be played with, examined and admired. The child wants to preserve and maintain what he or she has and identifies as their own – saying "it's mine". For example a found object such as a pebble, a feather or a twig and maybe even a favoured small toy will be squirreled away in the treasure box. Piaget calls this stage the age of concrete operations, where experiments about the material world take place and understanding is consolidated. Children at this stage play together in small groups. Gangs are formed with secret hideouts and passwords, dens are built and only the initiated are allowed in. New information is soaked up, the child talks with peers and adults alike, learns and uses new words and develops a growing sense of independence and confidence. By the time the end of this house is reached, the physical stage of pre-puberty begins.

The 3rd house – 12 to 18 years
Learning and education

In the 3rd house the focus is on puberty and growing up, set alongside the increasing demands coming from school and academic or practical work and study. Friendships are formed and some of them may include first steps into romantic liaisons. Alongside the challenges and demands of learning and the accompanying tests and examinations, the young adult begins to form ideas which are discussed in depth and at length with peers. Peer groups take precedence over family at this stage as the individual moves away from the safety of the parental home and feels more in tune with like-minded friends. Rebellion and more assertion of individuality takes place, often expressed through styles of clothing, such as cult dressing. The young adult identifies with pop groups and plays loud music. This stage is most likely to manifest between ages 15 and 16. Beyond this there is more focus on developing ideals, the will is formed and the young adult begins to have a sense of direction about their future and the career path they might take. There is a strengthening sense of individuality and purpose, and as the IC and age 18 is reached, the person prepares to leave the safety of the parental home and set out on their own journey in life.

The 2nd Quadrant: 4th, 5th and 6th houses

This Quadrant spans the IC to the DC, covering ages 18 to 36 years. It is associated with the element of Earth, and with instinctive behaviour, in the sense that we instinctively learn to adapt our behaviour so that we fit in. We learn to match our behaviour and responses to the expectations of the environment. It's the realm of the Unconscious "You" and its focus is on mastery of the environment.

The 4th house – 18 to 24 years
Moving away from the parental home

Adult age begins here, and in some cases it comes slightly earlier than this when the surge of energy around the IC and the 4th cusp is felt in the 3rd house, in the late teens, just ahead of the Age Point reaching this next cardinal point. At the IC, there is another huge surge of outward energy which gives the individual the momentum and motivation to move away from the safety of the parental nest and loosen the family ties. Instead of being part of the collective they have grown up in, the now adult seeks to make their own way in the world. At this stage, young adults move away and separate from the family home, perhaps to get married or live with a partner and experience new life situations. The world becomes their oyster and they don't want their style hampered as they extend their involvement with life.

The 5th house – 24 to 30 years
Testing our life experiences

The theme of the 2nd Quadrant is knowing how to fit in, behave, and respond in social situations of all kinds. This Quadrant is also associated with adapted behaviour. In houses 4, 5 and 6 we observe others and from them learn acceptable ways of behaving. In the 5th house this is especially so as we are on the front line of testing out our life experiences against those of others. It's the realm of learning how to get on with people and how to relate in a manner appropriate to the situation. The Hubers say, "This is one of the great phases of experience and learning." In the 5th house the focus is on building and maintaining personal and professional partnerships, with a view to securing these before moving into the 6th house where our existence has to be established and assured.

Prince William: 5th House Venus

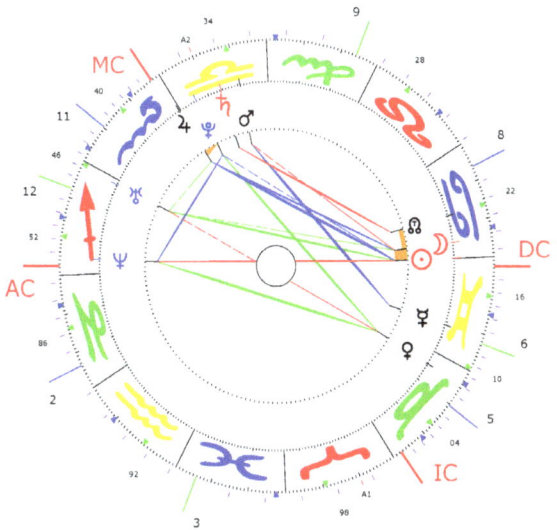

21.6.1982, 21:03, London, England

The chart of Prince William, the Duke of Cambridge, offers an example of a 5th house tenanted by just one planet – Venus – the planet whose psychological drive is for harmony and contact. When the energies of Venus are active and engaged with positively, we are able to relate to people and situations in our lives in a pleasant and friendly way, seeking rapport with those we meet. William is somewhat blessed to have this planet in the 5th house where, in his increasingly high profile role as a senior member of the British royal family, he is participating more actively in meeting people from all walks of life, and is expected to get on with them as part of the job. William's Age Point moved into the 6th house on his 30th birthday, but the groundwork for his role as future king has been laid down over the past 6 years, between ages 24 and 30, as he has established his presence, as a royal and an individual with a career as a rescue helicopter pilot, in anticipation of what will become his life, his work and his means of existence in the future.

The 6th house – 30 to 36 years
Coping with and establishing existence

This house is associated with work and service to fellow colleagues, and to finding our own place in life. It's not an area or house that is traditionally associated with fun; it's serious stuff in the workplace because our very existence depends upon making a success of life there. Those who haven't yet found their calling or vocation in life will be challenged to find it during this life phase, so will need to be assertive but also realistic about what can and cannot be achieved professionally. The closer the Age Point moves towards the DC and the 7th house, the more the orientation of interest changes to focus on this next psychological life phase. Like the AC and IC before it, the DC has a huge surge of energy, and in this case it's a very important one as it carries the individual from the lower, unconscious hemisphere of the chart to the upper hemisphere and the realm of consciousness. The Hubers call this phase a "vital peak in life".

Sarah: 6th House Focus

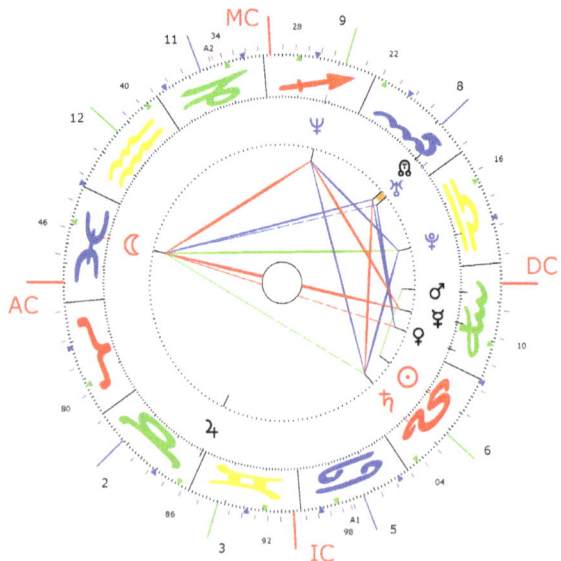

11.08.1976, 21:40, Crewe, England

Sarah is a professional woman with a strong focus of planets in the 6th house of her chart. Her job involves educating and training public sector health care professionals. Her Age Point is close to the DC, in the stress area before the 7th house cusp. Psychologically she is already anticipating the change from the lower to the upper hemisphere of the chart. Her focus of energy between ages 30 and 36, as her Age Point has travelled through the 6th house, has been on developing her career and on gaining related additional qualifications to support this. She has studied for a Master's degree alongside working full time, and has without doubt found the presence of the four planets in this house a supportive influence. Her Age Point is currently conjunct Mars and, like an athlete, she has put in the final spurt of energy to reach the finishing line and complete the writing of her dissertation, before the DC is reached and crossed.

The 3rd Quadrant: 7th, 8th and 9th Houses

This Quadrant spans the DC to the MC, covering ages 36 to 54 years. It is associated with the element of Air, and with wide awake thinking. This is the realm of the Conscious "You", where we acknowledge and consider what others want alongside what we want, sometimes putting the needs of others first. Its main theme is environment recognition because this is where we're in contact with others and have to be able to communicate successfully with them.

The 7th house – 36 to 42 years
Intense outward focus, relationships and partners

When the Age Point crosses the DC at 36 years it enters the upper, conscious hemisphere of the chart. This is often experienced as a time when the individual comes into their own and feels more empowered to take on new directions in life. In the 7th house the focus on relationships and one to one partnerships is strong. At this psychological stage our ability to make contact with others is at optimum strength. We also realise – often with some excitement – that there is so much more potential in life for us than we'd ever before dreamed of. Major decisions are made regarding the future and significant commitments undertaken. We can move forward on both the personal and professional front. At age 40 we may falter or pause as we take stock of life. Crises in partnerships and a revision of our lifestyle are possible challenges to be faced before we can move on towards the next house. The Hubers suggest that "the completion of character formation takes place around age 42".

Fred Astaire: 7th House Neptune

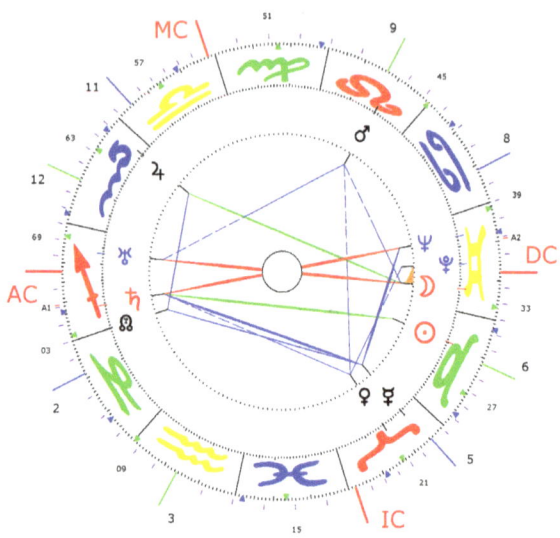

10.05.1899, 21:16, Omaha, Nebraska, USA

When the Age Point of dancer, actor and film star Fred Astaire was travelling through the 7th house in his chart, he was heavily involved in making the musical films with co-dancer Ginger Rogers, which made him famous. Not only did he perform in them, he also choreographed the dance routines. During this period, he also became involved with camera and filming techniques, introducing innovative new ideas about camera angles during the dance routines. Astaire was a very popular film star and his relationship with the public, through his films, was on a high at this time. Alongside this his professional development was moving forward as he choreographed and directed the filming of his impeccable dance routines. The presence of both Pluto and Neptune in Astaire's 7th house strengthen and intensify the events during this psychological phase. Notably his Age Point was conjunct Neptune when he became involved in filming techniques.

The 8th house – 42 to 48 years
Transformation, rebirth and the mid-life crisis
The 8th house is probably the most significant when considering Age Progression, and we will return to this house and look at it in greater detail later in the book. It's never an easy house to get to grips with in terms of really understanding what it means astrologically; for example, the blanket description of "death and rebirth" doesn't do it justice and should not be taken literally. The 8th house is psychologically more about major changes in the way we see and experience ourselves out in the world. In this period we may undergo many transformations. Our status will change. For example, we're perhaps suddenly no longer a needed parent but an empty-nester when offspring leave and move away from home. For stay-at-home parents this brings the new challenge of returning to work, or of finding a new career and/or a new orientation in life. There may be frustrations and a feeling of marking time while we decide which direction to head in next, and this is often accompanied by doubts and fears of what the new and unknown future may hold. Personal values may undergo a complete revision at this stage, as all that was previously considered important is pared down or changed forever.

The 9th house – 48 to 54 years
Formation of individual life philosophy.
Here we concerned with what is of true and lasting value, and we form our own philosophy of life. We may be challenged to stand alone and speak up for not only what we truly believe in, but for what we know for ourselves, based on our first-hand life experience to date. We may grapple with age-old questions such as "What is the meaning of my life? Where do I come from and where am I heading?" A deeper sense of meaning is often sought by exploring spiritual or philosophical matters and learning new approaches to how we live our life. New ideals are nurtured, but if the individual is not able to connect with these, or recall the ideals he or she had in youth, a crisis of meaning may result. This is a time of seeking and searching, where spiritual values are found or rediscovered, and are blended together with the life experiences and what the person knows to be true for themselves.

The 4th Quadrant: 10th, 11th and 12th Houses

This Quadrant spans the MC to the IC, covering ages 54 to 72 years. It's associated with the element Water, and with the act of simply being. This is the realm of the Conscious "I", where we can be self-realised and confident in ourselves as we are. We don't need to hold on to anything as we are comfortable with who and what we are in the here and now. We're able to share with others what we have learned from life, and we rest easy with this as we no longer need to impress anyone. The main theme for this Quadrant is self-awareness.

The 10th house – 54 to 60 years
Authority, individuation and self realisation

When we reach the 10th house and the MC, it's as though we have climbed a tree and are sat on the highest branches surveying the landscape of our lives spread out before us. It may feel quite isolated and vulnerable being "up high" and in a position where others look up to us, because of our experience, seniority and/or authority. We are expected to know things, to have made a success of our life so far, and it's during the 10th house that careers peak. In this house we're still riding on the outward surge of energy coming from the MC, but if we have no inner resources of strength, conviction and mature self-realisation to draw upon, life can feel lonely. It dawns upon us, as we move through the 10th house, that we are not irreplaceable. For some this will be accepted gracefully as we progress on to the next psychological life phase in the 11th house; for others who have much of their self image invested in always being right and being something of an authority, moving on to the next phase may be difficult.

The 11th house – 60 to 66 years
Freely chosen friends and relationships

In the 11th house we have the opportunity to sort out the wheat from the chaff as far as our friends and associates are concerned. We're able to differentiate easily between those who are true friends, and those who have been friendly because it profited them in some way. People we formed close relationships with in the opposite 5th house, when we were between the ages of 24 and 30, are more likely to remain; they are the friends we've relied on through the years. In this house, retirement age is reached or approaches. We have more time available to spend with our chosen friends, and it's important that we are mentally and/or physically engaged in other areas of interest so we don't suddenly find we have nothing meaningful to do. Joining with others of like mind we may seek to become involved in activities which benefit society as a whole. We have the free time and the skills to make important contributions at this stage, often working voluntarily to support charities or needy causes as we move through the Quadrant associated with sharing what we are good at to benefit others.

The 12th house – 66 to 72 years
Introversion, solitude

Moving into 12th house, we approach the run-up to completing one circuit of the chart. Here we no longer need to strive to prove anything to anyone, and this can be very liberating. As befits the qualities of the fourth Quadrant, we can truly be ourselves. Some high profile people choose to continue working into this phase, for example politicians, artists, musicians, writers, scientists, spiritual leaders. Others less prominent will continue on their chosen path in a less conspicuous way, working with what interests them and has meaning. They will carry forward the interest, impetus and desire to make a contribution to society, which began in the 11th house. Physically, life in 12th house may be more challenging as the body is less supple and more prone to illness, but with the maturity and self awareness that accompanies this phase, the individual can face such challenges with equanimity and wisdom. The Hubers say, "Those who were selfless, loving, just and generous will now be even more so; the difficult, egotistical, hard, bitter, petty, suspicious and argumentative will calcify along these lines."

As the Age Point crosses the AC at age 72 there is once again a huge surge or energy at this cardinal point to carry us forward anew into the 1st house. Here we have renewed energy and have returned to a place we knew and experienced before, but with the experiences of a lifetime to draw upon as we embark on this next phase, finding new meaning in everything we do.

Pablo Picasso: 10th House Focus

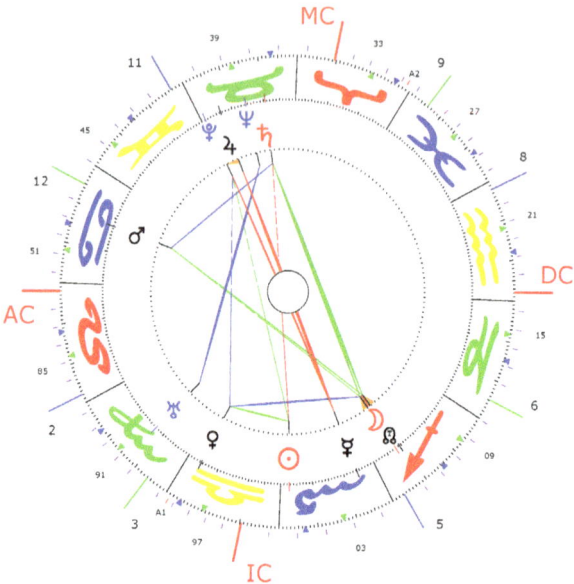

25.10.1881, 23:15, Malaga, Spain

The artist Pablo Picasso has a 10th house tenanted by four planets – Jupiter, Saturn, Neptune and Pluto – making it a focal point of output and expression in his chart at the time when he was at the peak of his career. As his Age Point moved through this house in the 1920's and 30's, his art was in what is known as his Classicism and Surrealism period. During this period he painted his most famous work, *Guernica*, a depiction of German bombing during the Spanish Civil War. Picasso continued to paint and produce etchings as his Age Point moved through the 11th and 12th houses, right up until his death in 1973, moving beyond the 12th house and into the first three houses once again.

Notes to Part 1 Age Progression and the Houses

*5 Stress Planets are discussed in detail in *Transformation: Astrology as a Spiritual Path* by Bruno & Louise Huber

*6 A brief introduction to Piaget's work can be found in *The Growth of Understanding in the Young Child* by Nathan Isaacs

Part 2

House Zones, Balance Point and Low Point

In this section we take a deeper and more detailed look at the Dynamic Energy Curve through the houses. The surge of energy at the four cardinal points of the chart, the AC, IC, DC and MC, is reflected in the smaller, corresponding surge at each house cusp. We will be taking a closer look at the Age Point's movement around this curve of energy, at the different zones or areas within each house and at the Balance and Low Points which are found there.

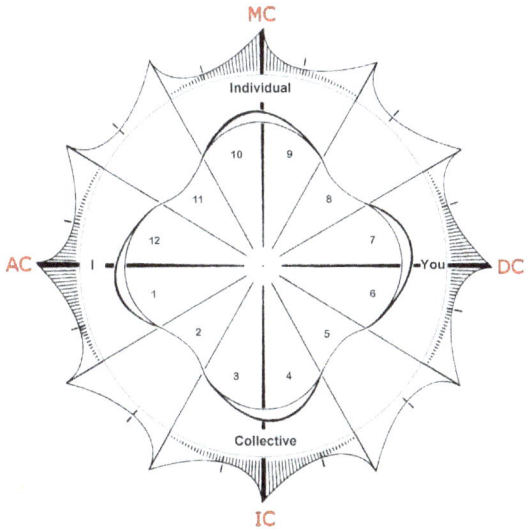

Dynamic Energy Curve

Cardinal, Fixed and Mutable Zones

The Dynamic Energy Curve displays a pattern of peaks and troughs as it flows around the chart. Starting at the AC, the Age Point moves in an anti-clockwise direction through the houses. At the cusp of each house the energy intensity peaks, but then gradually falls off until the Balance Point is reached at approximately one-third of the way into the house. The energy continues to diminish until it reaches its lowest ebb at the Low Point, approximately two-thirds of the way through the house.

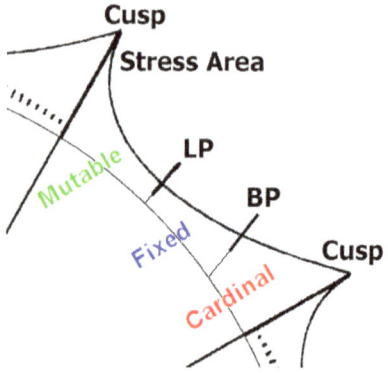

Cardinal, Fixed and Mutable Zones

The houses are thus divided into three distinct zones moving from cusp to cusp. The zone from the cusp to the Balance Point has a cardinal quality; from the Balance Point to the Low Point the quality is fixed, and between the Low Point and the next cusp the quality is mutable. As the Age Point moves through each house, subtle but distinct changes of behaviour and focus can be felt according to whether the Age Point is in a particular house zone or close to the Balance Point or Low Point.

If there is a planet present at any of these positions its expression will be modified. The role of the planets in Age Progression will be covered in depth in part 4.

The House Cusp and the Cardinal Zone

The house cusp can be likened to a mountain top, a pedestal, a high vantage point or the penthouse apartment with a view to go with it. When the Age Point is there the person will have a sense of being able to see clearly; a panoramic view of where they've come from and where they're heading for next can be seen from this position. There is a sense of excitement and anticipation, and a feeling that anything is possible. As the Age Point moves from the cusp to the Balance Point, life can feel exhilarating as the momentum of energy propels us forward, often quite fast. We can get things going, energy flows easily and we are spurred into action. It's the cardinal zone of the house where goals can be aimed for and achieved. We're in "doing" mode and the focus of energy is on activity and output.

Charles Dickens: Age Point in Cardinal Zone

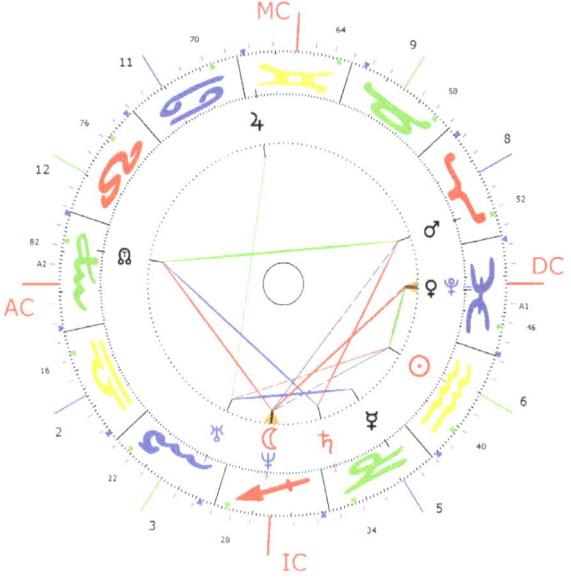

07.02.1812, 19:50, Portsmouth, England

The chart of Victorian novelist Charles Dickens gives an example of the Age Point in the cardinal zone. Dickens' works were a commentary on the Victorian times he was living in, and he criticised the social division between those who had more than they needed and those who were living in poverty. Dickens was a freelance journalist, who also became a parliamentary commentator. In 1836 his first novel, *The Pickwick Papers*, was published. At this time his Age Point was in the cardinal zone of the 5th house and conjunct Mercury, the planet associated with communication. This combination offers a graphic example of the Age Point conjunct a planet in the go-ahead cardinal zone. Mercury is in an excellent position in this house to be expressed effectively and to be noticed. What is said will be heard and recognised, enabling Mercury to have its say with ease. All this is reinforced by the passage of the Age Point through the activity-oriented cardinal zone.

The Balance Point

Approximately one-third of the way through the house the Balance Point is reached. The energy curve has smoothed out a little and what might have felt like an exhilarating dash down a ski slope now levels off into something more measured. At the Balance Point there is more equilibrium. We don't need to be quite so active here because the available energy coming to us from within the chart is in balance with the demands made by the outside world. At the Balance Point it's as though we can handle whatever comes our way with poise, skill and confidence. Life may still be busy and active, but we're able to take this in our stride. We are in balance, and we do not need to give out more energy than is required. Things are easier, smoother and more efficient. Energy is harnessed and channelled towards the task in hand, which can be undertaken in an apparently effortless way. The time the Age Point takes to travel from the cusp to the Balance Point is 2 years and 3 months.

Sally: Age Point on Balance Point

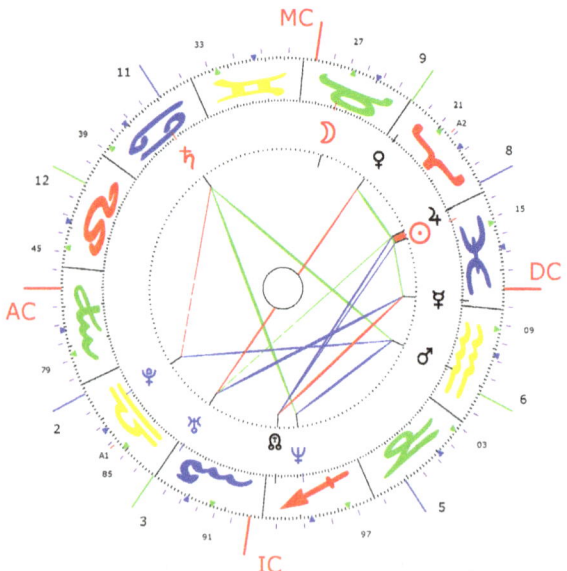

17.03.1975, 17:05, Nuneaton, England

Sally gave birth to her son when her Age Point was on the Balance Point in the 6th house. He was her first child and up until this time she had been working full time as a solicitor. She stopped work just before her baby was due, when she was involved with a murder case.

She calmly took this in her stride. With her Age Point moving through the 6th house, the focus of her energy had been on her professional life, in line with the psychological phase of establishing her presence in the workplace, the theme of this house. The birth was easy and straightforward. Sally went into labour and then to hospital to have her baby, who was born in the early hours of the morning. She was back at home by the evening of the same day, having spent less than 24 hours in hospital. She was very calm and composed, having a quick and easy birth and a speedy return to her home environment. With her Age Point on the Balance Point, the output of energy demanded of her, first professionally by her work, and then personally when she gave birth, were congruent with the available energy she had coming from within. At the time of her son's birth, the Age Point was also making a square aspect to her unaspected Moon, creating an important link to her feelings and emotional sense of self. An Age Point aspect to the Moon is a classic significator in any event which has a high emotional charge, and is frequently found in a woman's chart when she gives birth.

The Fixed Zone

The area between the Balance Point and the Low Point is where the energy curve flattens out. The motivation here is to stay put, preserve the status quo as much as possible, and keep things pretty much as they are. With the Age Point in this fixed zone the aim is to hang on to what is known, safe and secure. Someone with the Age Point in the fixed zone of a house is likely to assume a fixed stance, which may be quite firmly held. They will not want to move forward or take risks and will be content to mark time for a while, consolidating what has gone before.

The Low Point

The time taken by the Age Point to travel from the cusp to the Low Point is 3 years and 8 months. Here, the Dynamic Energy Curve is at its lowest ebb. In the context of its flowing pattern of peaks and troughs, at the Low Point it reaches rock bottom. Arriving at a Low Point is an important and significant psychological stage. When the Low Point in each house is reached this is the time when inner reflection is called for. The individual can take stock of all the life experiences which have gone before, and can reconnect with the circle in the centre of the chart where the personal and transpersonal self meet. In the outside world it will be more of an effort for the person to summon up the drive and energy required to participate effectively in the affairs of the house concerned. At the Low Point the motivation and available energy become much more introspective as the person turns their attention to the inner life and what is going on inside. Louise Huber has likened the Low Point experience to being closer to the soul's purpose. It's when we begin to question everything we have done so far and start looking for new meaning in our personal, professional and spiritual life. Rather than the Age Point moving into the Low Point being a cause of fear and dread – which it might be for those who do not understand what is happening – it can bring a welcome period of quiet inner reflection and be just the kick we needed to propel us into taking stock of life and making major decisions and changes. At the Low Point we pause. It's like a crossroads complete with signposts – which way next? The same, familiar route we know? Or something different which will open us up to new experiences and horizons?

Mid-Life Crisis

Trained consultants working with astrological psychology often find that clients will seek help and clarification about their life journey when they reach a Low Point. It has been my experience that time and again people come when their Age Point is on a Low Point. Quite often this is at the 8th house Low Point. When we move through the 8th house the need is felt to completely reassess our lifestyle, particularly when we're at the age related to this Low Point – age 45 to 46. Low Point 8 is, in astrological psychology, the "big one" which relates closely to the mid-life crisis, and it is also the Low Point of the whole chart. The psychological life phase associated with the 8th house is one of rebirth and transformation. At Low Point 8 many people change jobs, some leave the relationship they're in while others consider more generally what they are doing with the rest of their lives and ask if they want to continue in the same way. It can be a time to shed the old and create anew. The experience of the Low Point and the period of introspection which goes with it may last for anything up to a year, and it can begin up to eight months beforehand. Rather like the sound of a gong rising to a crescendo and then fading away, the Low Point experience is one which builds quite slowly and then gradually subsides when the Age Point moves on. In this period of time the self-aware individual has the opportunity to recognise, acknowledge and accept that some changes may have to be made, together with the chance to start anew at this psychological crossroads.

Philip: Age Point on Low Point

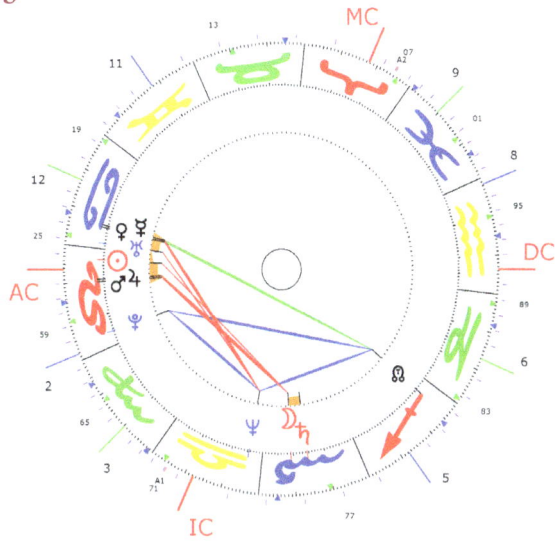

27.07.1955, 05:30, Hull, England

Philip came to see me as a client seeking guidance and clarification on where he was going in his life when his Age Point was on Low Point 8 and he was 45. I'd already noted that his current Age Point could be significant when I did my preparatory work on his chart. It's a very "I" sided chart, with no less than six planets, including the Sun, clustered around the AC area. The overall aspect structure nestles predominantly into the 1st Quadrant leaving a large open and vulnerable space covering houses 6 to 12. This would give Philip little protection from the "You", so I expected him to be a rather private person, maybe shy or reclusive and possibly preferring his own company. Looking at this alongside the position of his Age Point on Low Point 8 – the Low Point of the whole chart – I needed to be sensitive to how he might want to explore the issues he'd brought with him. I was aware of the potential significance of the Small Talent triangle in his chart, pinned by transpersonal planets Neptune and Pluto and the Moon's Node, which itself can act like a signpost and lead to greater self-awareness. I'd noted that Neptune, at the apex of the Talent triangle, was the lowest planet in the chart and was strongly placed in the cardinal zone of the 4th house, where it could be directed to work effectively within the community, possibly in a caring role. I'd speculated that he could be drawn towards some kind of pastoral care work, and during our session he told me he sensed that he had a specific task. He'd considered going in to the priesthood.

At age 42, with his Age Point making a quincunx to Uranus as it entered the 8th house, Philip's wife had died, leaving him to care for their 9 year old daughter. Over the last few years he'd had Cruse counselling for the bereaved, which had awakened in him an interest in psychotherapy and self-understanding. At the time of the session, the next planet his Age Point would contact, by a trine aspect, was Saturn. One of the things Philip wanted to look at in the session was his lack of grounding. He felt that he had plenty of ideas, but no action to go with them. Saturn is at the bottom of the chart, in the 4th house, and conjunct the Moon. Both these planets are in Scorpio, itself deep and intense, and the sign is intercepted. Any deep and intense feelings Philip had, and might bottle up, would struggle to be expressed satisfactorily for him out in the world. At Low Point 8, this was all coming to a head as he realised that part of his current dilemma included finding a way to channel his true feelings and the ideas he had so they could be heard and acknowledged out in the world.

Noting that his Leo Sun was in the mutable zone of the 12th house, and was in a stressed position close to the cusp, it became clear that giving some attention to developing the Sun – his will – was important. The Sun in the middle of the large stellium could provide an important outlet for his Moon/Saturn. Linked by a square aspect, the first job in hand was to strengthen the Sun by developing his will, and to get that square aspect working, so that the intercepted planets could have a voice.

The Mutable Zone

The area between the Low Point and the upcoming cusp is the mutable zone, where the energy curve begins to pick up again. If the Low Point symbolises the lowest ebb of energy in the Dynamic Curve, its movement through the mutable zone of the house signifies a steady picking up and increase of energy as the cusp is approached. Moving from Low Point to cusp can be likened to walking uphill, climbing a long flight of stairs or even a mountain. There is hard work and effort involved but the motivation is there to reach the top. There's a goal to be aimed for and we emerge from the Low Point with renewed vigour and often a completely new outlook on life. This house zone has mutable, changeable qualities. We may have to be more psychologically flexible as we consciously aim for where we're heading. All may not go according to plan so we have to adapt and go with the changing energy flow, but always moving onwards and upwards, towards the cusp and the next house with its different qualities and associated psychological life phase.

The Stress Area

Everything may be going swimmingly at first as we move through the mutable zone, but then things can start to get a bit sticky. The momentum of energy which started us on this journey to the cusp comes under more and more pressure the closer we get to the cusp. Rather like the climb up the hill, the mountain or the flight of stairs, we can get puffed out, need a rest, or perhaps find the whole thing too daunting. We may want to give up, or wish – in the case of the stairs – we'd had the sense to take the lift. At this point we need to exert even more energy to reach our goal, and here I'm talking about the psychological goal of reaching the next house/area of life experience, not the physical one of reaching the mountain top, although they do have similarities. There is a sense of stress and expectation and we have to summon up reserves of additional energy to make the final push which will take us to the mountain top. Likewise with life, we have to put out more energy than we have readily available and this can be draining and exhausting. If we have planets in this area, they will be under a lot of pressure to perform out in the world; they are called Stress Planets. We will look more closely at such planets in a later section of the book.

The journey of the Age Point through the house, from cusp to cusp, is now complete. Once the stress area has been navigated, the Age Point arrives at the cusp of the next house, and once again its position can be likened to being on a mountain top, a pedestal, a high vantage point, or in a penthouse apartment with a view.

Psychological View of Houses

It's important to be aware, however, that psychologically, the move towards the next house begins before the cusp is reached. Psychologically the houses run from Low Point to Low Point. So when the Age Point is in the 5th house, the change of focus and interest in 6th house matters begins at Low Point 5, when the person is around 27 to 28 years old. The orientation of the individual towards 6th house matters starts here and is already in operation well before the 6th cusp is reached at age 30.

Size of House

The speed of the Age Point is constant and it always moves at a rate of 6 years per house. However, the size of the house it's moving through has to be considered. If it's travelling through a small house, the Age Point moves slowly. This experience can be quite intense as events will make a deeper and longer-lasting impression on the individual during this period of time. There is plenty of time for life experiences to be savoured and for them to make a lasting impression.

When travelling through a large house, the Age Point seems to move faster and it can feel as though there's plenty going on. Life will be busy, sometimes verging on hectic. Although the individual may experience more things happening, these events will be touched on in less depth and with less intensity as there is less time for them to make an impression. In a large house it is as though the Age Point is skating through at top speed, hardly pausing before the next event comes along.

Empty Houses and Open Spaces

In addition to noting the aspects that the Age Point makes to planets in the chart, open spaces in the overall aspect structure should also be taken into consideration. These spaces can be deceptive as they give an initial impression that nothing much is likely to be happening as the Age Point moves through them. However, don't be fooled by this! With Age Progression, something is always happening. The psychological life phases, the size of the houses, the sign changes and the movement of the Age Point across the Balance Points, Low Points and house cusps, together with any aspects to planets that the Age Point makes as it transits this open space could prove this initially uninteresting open space to be crammed full of activity.

Laura: Empty 'You' Side

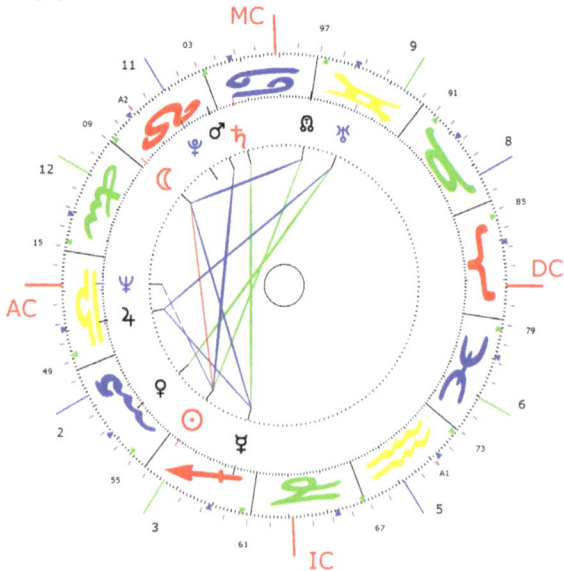

26.11.1945, 02:30, London, England

Laura's chart is very strongly "I" sided, leaving almost the entire "You" side of her chart empty. The central core of the chart is also vulnerable and exposed, being unprotected by aspects. She can find that others seem to come on a bit too strong, so she will sometimes need to retreat and spend time on her own, or be with people she feels comfortable with. Houses 4 to 8 are empty, yet in this period of time she had an interesting and varied career, first as a teacher and then as an officer in the merchant navy. This enabled her to travel around the world several times and visit exotic places, meeting the man she married along the way, starting her own family and eventually returning to full time teaching where she held a position of considerable responsibility.

Using Age Progression, these events are reflected in the houses and psychological life phases she was moving through at the time, with the signs offering a significant and appropriate backdrop. When she was at sea and travelling her Age Point was moving through the 5th house, where life experiences and relationships are tested out, and it was also in the freedom-loving sign of Aquarius. When her Age Point was in the 6th house she got married and had her family, these events coinciding with a change of sign to Pisces. With her Age Point in the 6th house she began to build up her career, initially working part-time to fit in with her family commitments. When her Age Point crossed the DC and entered the 7th house, it had already moved into the more outgoing and energetic sign of Aries. This coincided with an increased emphasis on teaching, and an eventual move from part-time to full time work. Her career was established as her Age Point moved through practical, down to earth Taurus and the 8th house, and for many years she was head of the nursery department in the school where she taught. Throughout this period of time, her Age Point was making numerous aspects to the planets occupying the "I" side of the chart. Aspects to planets and their significance in Age Progression are covered in depth in part 4.

The brief overview of Laura's chart given here demonstrates how the movement of the Age Point through the empty houses correlates closely with her life experience. A detailed analysis, taking all these factors into consideration, along with the other techniques used in Age Progression, would demonstrate how, with this method of timing in the horoscope, something is always going on.

In the next section we will look at the movement of the Age Point through the signs. These form an important backdrop to the psychological life phases and can colour our experiences in a specific way.

Part 3

Age Progression and the Signs

As the Age point moves around the chart passing from house to house and moving through the psychological life phases already described, it also travels through the twelve zodiac signs. Each sign has an underlying quality relating to the element it represents. The sign and its quality form a backdrop which colours the setting and nature of the life experiences. When the Age Point changes from one sign to the next as it travels around the chart, this also brings a corresponding change in the quality of the psychological life experiences of the individual.

Fire Signs

Fire signs are eager, active, warm, outgoing and initiatory. If you bring to mind what an actual fire looks, feels and sounds like, you will probably be able to think of some words to describe it. These, to give a few examples, may be wildfire, heat, blaze, flare, spark, ignite, kindle, inflame, roar… and you can probably think of plenty more yourself. All of these words are descriptive of the element of Fire, and when the Age Point is moving through a Fire sign, it is these qualities which are likely to be more accessible.

Staying with the stage backdrop analogy, when the Age Point moves through a Fire sign it can feel to the individual as if he or she has walked on to a stage set where there is a lot of enthusiastic activity taking place. It's a place full of buzz, where things are physically being undertaken, and lively productivity is in process. There's no time to sit and rest because the fiery nature of the energy keeps things in motion and constantly initiates new projects. However, when the Age Point moves into the next sign – an Earth sign – there is a change of energy from intense activity towards completion and consolidation.

Earth Signs

Earth signs have a very different quality. They are more solid, more practical and more sensual. They have more time, too, to sit and rest as they do not carry the same energetic charge as the Fire signs. Their energy is focussed on conserving and consolidating, and on the completion of projects. They are attuned to substance and form and are endowed with an earthy practicality which makes them steadier and somewhat slower in their approach. If the Fire signs are like the hare, the Earth signs are most certainly like the tortoise! This is not to say they are always slow; they just take their time, they're more thorough and are concerned first and foremost with the material.

When the Age Point changes from a Fire to an Earth sign life can take on a slower pace and flavour. The individual with the Age Point moving into an Earth sign will feel as if they have walked on to a stage set where there is less frenzied activity and more evidence of steadiness. Preservation and maintenance will be of importance here, along with laying down firm foundations and executing planned activities. The excited buzz of Fire changes to a sure and steady background hum as things slow down. After a while though, this can start to feel heavy. People with the Age Point moving towards the end of an Earth sign speak of it as being like wading through mud in mud-caked wellington boots. Life starts to feel like hard work and the upcoming change from an Earth to an Air sign is something of a welcome relief.

Air Signs

Air signs are concerned with communication and the circulation of ideas, thoughts, words, gestures and often intangible "airy" things which can't be pinned down. Air signs like nothing better than communicating, riding the airwaves or internet, expressing their views and picking up interesting snippets from others along the way. They don't like to be pinned down and enjoy freedom of expression. They can range far and wide, seeking out what interests them.

When the Age Point changes from an Earth to an Air sign a sense of lightening up will be experienced. The heaviness of the Earth sign that has been travelled through gives way to a welcome sense of lightness. There is less emphasis on practical matters and more on communication and learning. The individual with the Age Point entering an Air sign will feel as if they have arrived on a stage set crammed full of a variety of new opportunities to communicate using many different methods. There could be an intangible feeling of excitement at the many forms of mental stimulation available, such as books, mixed media resources, and new subjects to explore and learn about. Gone is the earthy heaviness, and it's replaced by the potential of what this airy phase holds. When the Age Point subsequently changes sign again, moving into a Water sign, the emphasis will change too and the focus will be upon feelings.

Water Signs

Water signs are sensitive and are led by their emotions. These can run deep and be very powerful. There is a fluidity to the quality of all the Water signs, and a perceptiveness which opens up an understanding of what others might be experiencing. Water signs can show empathy, but they are also able to connect with the intensity of their own feelings and express them. Depending on which Water sign is involved, the way this is done will not always be consistent. For example, Scorpio – the Fixed Water sign – will express its emotional sensitivity in a different manner to Pisces – the Mutable Water sign.

When the Age Point changes from an Air to a Water sign there could be a noticeable difference in outlook for the individual concerned. No longer will the stimulating airy stuff of ideas take precedence because emotions and feelings will have moved into the lead. The backdrop or stage set, which has previously focussed on the mind and the head stuff, switches round to focus on the realm of the heart. The individual becomes more aware of their emotional nature, and life experiences are imbued with greater sensitivity. When the Age Point changes from a Water to a Fire sign, this will signal a return to the more initiatory pattern.

Examples of the Age Point in the Elements

Age Point changing from Fire to Earth

I was resident astrologer for several years on BBC local radio, and during my regular slot I did charts live on air for people who called in to the studio. This was a phone-in programme and it was a challenging experience. I never knew what people were going to ask me or what might come up in this live phone-in, but I had great confidence in the various astrological psychology techniques I had at my disposal. The nature of a phone-in programme is very fast, and I had to think on my feet and be prepared to respond immediately. In this situation, Age Progression was a technique that I used often, and it never let me down. Age Progression, when described in a general way, can be relied upon to offer something of relevance about a particular time in their life for the person concerned; using it more specifically in a chart where the data is accurate, it can offer much more.

Michael: Fire to Earth

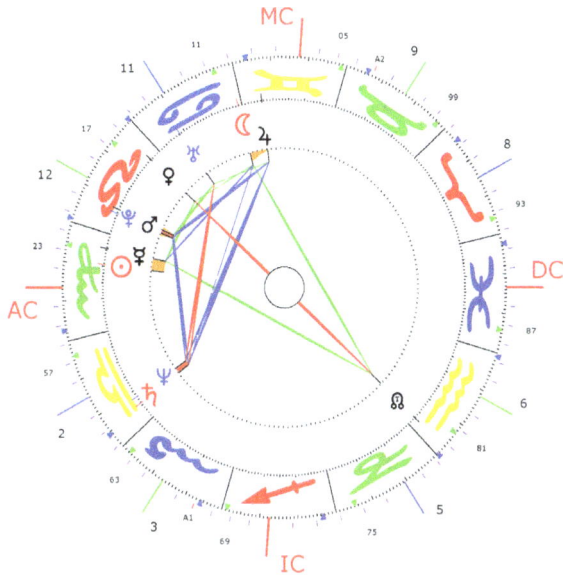

02.09.1953, 07:00, London, England

Michael called into the programme and wanted to know what I could see in his chart (he'd provided his data in advance of the programme so I had his chart to refer to). I noted that his chart resembled a paper aeroplane, and that he had a Virgo Sun, two Ear/Eye aspect patterns, a strong Small Talent triangle and a less-common Striving figure. Overall his chart had predominantly green/blue aspects and was lacking in red aspects. I was also aware that with the very red/green Striving figure, and the Virgo Sun, he could be quite a sensitive person. I knew I had to handle this interaction with kid gloves.

I asked him if he ran out of energy pretty quickly and needed time to recoup this energy loss because of his lack of red aspects, and he agreed. We talked about his Sun in Virgo and his possible perfectionist/nitpicking traits and he related well to this. Then he asked if there were better times coming up ahead, saying that he'd lost both his wife and son over the past two years.

This was quite a bombshell to drop, live on air, and I had to respond to this sensitively and sympathetically as well as swiftly – air time for each caller was always limited. I immediately used Age Progression to help me get a fix on where he was currently by age in the chart. His Age Point was in the 9th house, where there are no planets, but I referred back to the time he was talking about – the past two years. Even though there are also no planets in the 8th house, I was able to talk in general terms about the period of life between ages 42 and 48, saying that it was often experienced as a testing and transformative time. I was aware, too, that during this time his Age Point had changed from a Fire to an Earth sign.

I explained a few general things connected with the 9th house psychological phase, but concentrated on the sign his Age Point was now in – Taurus. I was able to say something about the solidity of this Earth sign as the back drop for his current life experience, together with the potential that was around for putting down new roots, using his creativity and looking for consolidation and stability in his life after the traumatic upheaval he had gone through. I also suggested that he probably had "bags of talent", drawing on the presence of the Small Talent triangle in his chart.

Age Point changing from Earth to Air

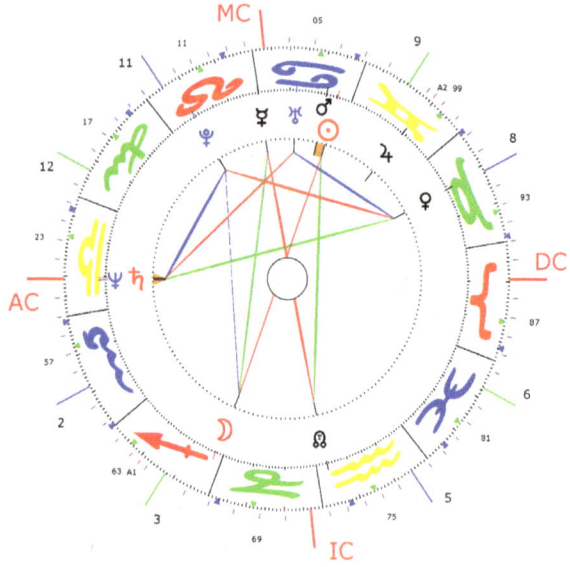

26.06.1953, 15.00, St. Ives, Cornwall, England

Sybille: Earth to Air

Sybille's chart has the appearance of someone walking carefully on two legs – maybe on stilts or on a tightrope – whilst carrying a large horizontal balancing pole to help keep them upright. Hers is a chart with a high ratio of red and green aspects. There are some blue aspects which will offer time to rest, consolidate and enjoy what has been worked for, but overall she will be an active and rather sensitive person with a lot of nervous energy to burn.

Sybille's experience of her Age Point changing from an Earth to an Air sign when she was 44 was not easy, but was ultimately positive. Whilst her Age Point had travelled through Taurus, life had been challenging – her sister had died and her marriage had ended. She says she worked very hard for 18 months to save her marriage and the business she shared with her husband before finally deciding to leave. As her Age Point moved towards the end of the Earth sign she felt the going was heavy. She was determined to prove she could stick at her marriage and make it work as she moved with dogged perseverance towards the next sign change.

When the Age Point moved into the Air sign of Gemini at age 44, her life changed quite dramatically. She left her marriage and lost many of the things she had valued. The move into an Air sign brought a real fear of being committed to any full time job, mortgage, or anything involving a major work commitment, and she had an intermittent love affair with a Norwegian woodsman/Venezuelan gold panner of no fixed abode and began to learn Norwegian. She also had a variety of part time jobs including care work, wood work and restaurant work and says she was pleased that every day was different.

Moving through an Air sign also opened up new possibilities for her, all of them connected in some way with words, communicating, learning new things and networking. She embarked on a counselling course and qualified as a counsellor, and she started to learn about subjects she was interested in, but had never studied before, such as biodiversity. She became passionately involved in an environmental project, so needed to find out about various aspects of maintaining a piece of local woodland. New areas of study and interest included discovering more about plants and lichens, butterflies and birds. She also had to learn how to create a website connected with this project, so that it could be publicised. All the new information and knowledge she acquired during this period was imbued with the airy energy of the sign, Gemini, and it is interesting to note that she has unaspected Jupiter in this sign. Without a doubt, the presence of Jupiter would have encouraged her to widen her interests and skills, and increase her understanding of all that she was involved in at that time.

Age Point changing from Air to Water

Author's Chart: Air to Water

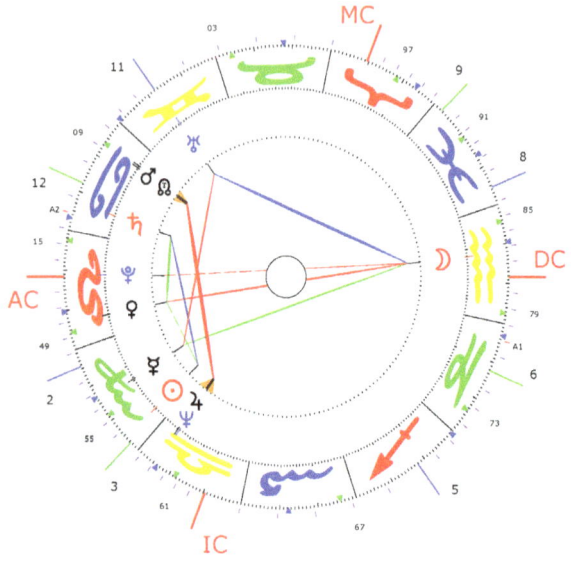

19.09.1945, 02:30, Tadcaster, England

I've often described my own chart as looking like a space capsule flying horizontally towards the Moon. I have a strongly "I" sided chart and a high ratio of red aspects, so I can be busy and active, sometimes finding it hard to switch off, relax and take time out for myself. The change of sign from Air to Water in my chart provides a recent example of the Age Point moving into a new sign and element. In 2004, soon after my Age Point entered Gemini, my co-authored first book on astrological psychology was published. Uranus is appropriately, and helpfully, strongly placed on the 11th cusp in this sign. This marked a new phase in my career as an astrologer as I shared, in the book, my teaching and consulting experience in this subject. I continued to write and teach as my Age Point progressed through this Air sign, but when in 2007 it moved into the Water sign of Cancer, I experienced a subtle but marked change in outlook.

My son and his wife moved overseas to live and work and suddenly a branch of my closest family were several thousand miles and a 10 hour flight away. I missed them and I realised that it was important to work at nurturing and sustaining close family ties in new and different ways in between our meetings. My family and my feelings about them have formed the backdrop of my current experiences and continue to do so now, especially since the birth of my first grandchild in 2009, when my Age Point was conjunct Mars and the Moon's Node. Family very much comes first right now as my Age Point progresses through this Water sign. Although I'm still writing – bringing the energy and experiences of my Age Point in Gemini with me – I'm more closely attuned to the sensitive, feeling flavour of the Water sign I'm in now.

Age Point changing from Water to Fire

Gareth: Water to Fire

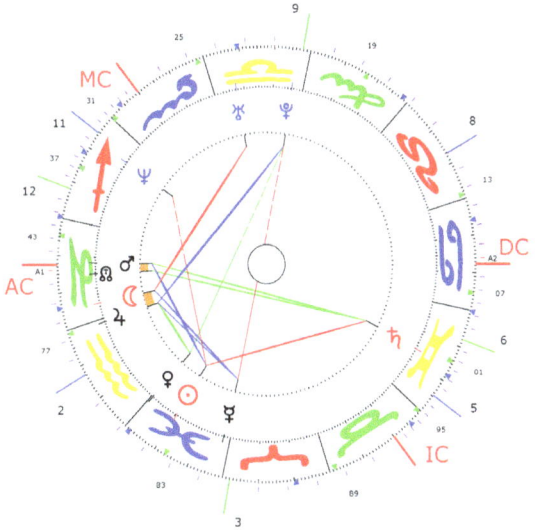

01.03.1973, 04:45, Crewe, England

Gareth's chart resembles the open beak of a bird, hungry and eager, but with an exposed and unguarded central core which can at times make him feel vulnerable. With most planets on the "I" side of the chart he can be reserved and initially cautious when meeting new people. He has a slightly high ratio of red and green aspects, with less blue, so time to relax and enjoy life is valuable and may have to be worked at.

Gareth's Age Point entered the Water sign of Cancer shortly after his 32nd birthday in 2005. This was also the year he got married, and making this commitment was important and significant for him. His Sun, Mercury and Venus, also in a Water sign, reflected the backdrop of feelings and sensitivity as his Age Point travelled through watery

Cancer. Events and experiences during the psychological life phase associated with the 6th house have also been in evidence. He's been establishing himself in his field of work, focussing on developing his career, and he's travelled quite extensively in his job.

At the time of writing, his Age Point is about to move into the Fire sign of Leo. There is a tangible sense of new opportunities around for him, and a fresh start to be made as the change from a Water to a Fire sign approaches, together with a feeling of many more possibilities opening up. It's an exciting and optimistic time. After a spell of moving around to different locations and living in different places, he is preparing to settle down for a while as he upgrades from owning a small apartment to buying a much larger house for his family.

Summary

It would be easy to dismiss the significance of the Age Point moving through the signs and changing from one sign to the next, in favour of focussing on some of the more "meaty" and obvious aspects of Age Progression. But to do this would be to lose out on important information. Sometimes, when the Age Point has no aspects to planets, and an exploration of the psychological life phase doesn't really answer some of the questions posed by a client, a look at the sign and its element will prove to be of great significance.

If you are using Age Progression, either for yourself or when looking at the chart of a friend, family member or client, it's always wise to include all features of this technique to ensure that you – and your client – get the most out of it.

Part 4

Age Progression and Aspects to Planets

So far, Age Progression and the movement of the Age Point has been looked at in the context of its journey through the houses and signs in the chart. The significance of the Dynamic Energy Curve in the houses has been considered and the importance of the house zones and the Balance and Low Points within the houses has been described. Now we come to the next levels of the chart – the inner areas where the planets and their aspects are found.

The aspect structure as a whole can give a great deal of information about the person. Is the overall structure composed of four or more sides? If so, it is quadrilateral, indicating that the inner and often unconscious motivation of the person has a predominantly fixed quality. If it is triangular in shape, the motivation will be mutable. If there are no quadrangular or triangular shapes present, but incomplete shapes and disconnected, tangential lines, the motivation will be cardinal. Chart shaping and motivation are described in my co-authored book *The Cosmic Egg Timer*.

Aspects made by the Age Point to the planets are highly significant, and it is to these that your eyes will fly when you've tried out the technique of Age Progression for a while and have gained a practical working understanding of it. The conjunction and opposition aspects are the strongest and generally have the greatest impact. The square and quincunx can also be very powerful and are hard to ignore. The trine, sextile and semi-sextile mostly have less impact and can be more subtle, but they form part of the cycle of Age Progression which begins with the conjunction to a planet, then moves on to make a semi-sextile, sextile, square, trine and quincunx to the planet before reaching opposition. The cycle then continues, but with the aspects made to the planet in reverse order until conjunction is reached again.

This cycle of aspects is illustrated by imagining the Age Point moving around the well-known Ptolemaic diagram from the point of conjunction.

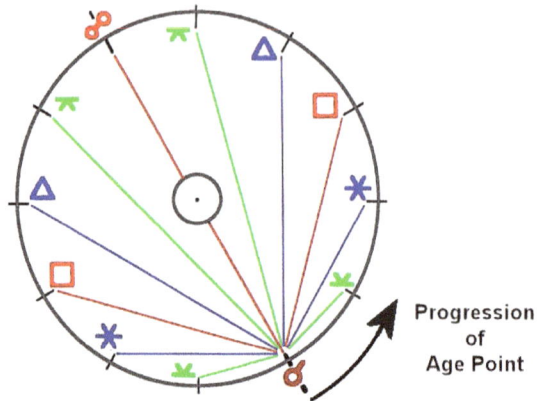

Cycle of Aspects made by the Age Point

All aspects made by the Age Point should be taken into consideration since every person and their experience of life, and of Age Progression, is different. When the Age Point aspects a planet, the energy and quality of that planet will colour the experience of the individual, bringing it more clearly into focus in their life at that time. For example, if the Age Point is making one of the stronger aspects to Mercury – let's say an opposition – then all the qualities and manifestations we associate with that planet will be poised in readiness to be experienced and expressed by the person concerned. Mercurial matters of all kinds will tend to dominate at this time.

Timing and Intensity

There is a preparatory period of influence for all Age Point aspects as their approach nears. This can be likened to the sound of a gong, which starts quietly, builds up to a crescendo of noise, and then dies away. Another analogy using sound is that of an emergency vehicle siren which can first be heard in the distance, becomes deafening as the vehicle passes by, but then subsides as it moves away. The approaching influence of an Age Point aspect can be felt some time ahead of the exact point in time when the aspect occurs. The person will have a sense of issues and matters which they would not normally be concerned with gradually demanding attention and taking prominence in their lives. This will be coloured by the qualities and characteristics of the planet involved. As each individual is different, it's not possible to say exactly how long the Age Point transit will last, but generally speaking the more aware the person is, and the better they know and understand themselves, the easier it will be to ride the impact and influence of the Age Point. As with the sounding of the gong and the passing of the emergency vehicle siren, after the approach the intensity of the Age Point transit begins to ease off. Once we are on the other side of an Age Point experience and the intensity has passed, it's very often only then that we are really able to understand what it was all about.

The size of the house involved will influence the experience of the Age Point's connection with a planet. In a large house, the movement of the Age Point is quick, so any aspect made to a planet as it travels through that house will be of less intensity. In a small house the opposite will be true as the Age Point will have more time to linger, and the involvement will be more intense.

Age Point in Conjunction

Conjunctions give an immediate, strong, direct and total taste of the qualities of the planet involved because we are literally eyeball to eyeball with it; there is no way of avoiding this encounter. The conjunction aspect brings a close, binding intensity, along with the potential for something new to emerge from this contact. When the Age Point is conjunct a planet, the drives associated with that planet are going to figure strongly in the person's life, and will come into sharp focus, perhaps blocking out other things for a brief period of time. There will be reminders and connections with the planet all around, and what it symbolises will seem to pop up in some form or another wherever we look. The experience of the Age Point conjunct a planet can feel like a complete immersion in the qualities of that planet, and for the individual it's an opportunity to more fully understand, experience and express that aspect of him or herself, both on an internal, psychological level and in what's happening in the immediate environment. Conjunctions, as well as emphasising the qualities of the planet involved, also bring into play the aspect pattern they are in, and will activate the other pinning planets in that pattern.

Charles Dickens: Age Point Conjunct Mercury

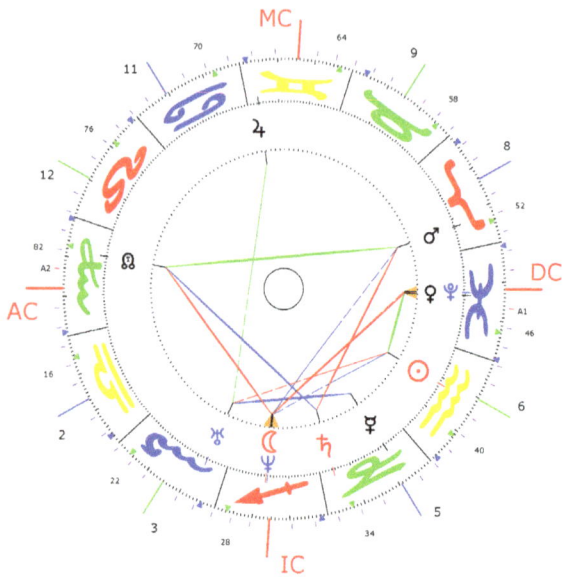

07.02.1812, 19:50, Portsmouth, England

Dickens' chart has already been used in Part 2 as an example of the Age Point in the cardinal zone of a house, where it also makes a conjunction with Mercury.

Dickens' work as a freelance journalist and parliamentary commentator helped lay the foundations of his career as a writer as he was already using and perfecting his expression of Mercury. Prior to the Age Point's conjunction with Mercury, Dickens was engaged in writing serialised sketches in periodicals which were published in 1836 under the title *Sketches by Boz*. This year was a significant one for Dickens. He married Caroline, daughter of George Hogarth, who was editor of the *Evening Chronicle*, and the publisher of *Sketches by Boz*. And it was then, as his Age Point was conjunct Mercury in 1836, that his first novel, *The Pickwick Papers*, was published. In this same year Dickens also became editor of another periodical, his career as a writer taking off with the publication of *The Pickwick Papers*. As we saw previously, Mercury, the planet associated with the drive to communicate, is very strongly placed in Dickens' chart. Just past the 5th cusp, it's in an excellent position to be heard, recognised and to have its say in the area of life associated with creativity, recreation and social awareness. In Victorian times, reading novels, periodicals and serialised stories (the "penny dreadfuls") was something of a leisure activity, and Dickens was able to capitalise on this interest.

Mercury is part of the linear zig-zagging aspect configuration in the chart and the conjunction of the Age Point lights up these other parts of the chart. Mercury connects by sextile to inventive, creative, forward-looking Uranus, which in turn squares Dickens' Sun. The Sun represents the use of the will, the mind, and creative thought and ideas as well as the sense of self. It is part of the small Learning triangle pinned by strongly placed Venus/Pluto and Moon/Neptune. This is quite a powerful combination. And if this were not enough, Uranus is quincunx Jupiter, their linear connecting aspect reaching right to the top of the chart with Jupiter looking like a hand held up high for all to see. Here in this configuration, and without too much stretching of the imagination, it is possible to see Dickens' skill as a writer concerned with social inequality working alongside his role as a campaigner against the slave trade, which took him to America and Canada.

Through his novels Dickens raised public awareness of injustice and inequality, voicing his concerns about the social deprivations of the time. He was also a philanthropist, raising funds for Great Ormond Street Hospital in London. Drawing on the energies of his strongly placed Mercury again, he raised money for charitable causes by giving public readings from his books. He also set up a home for "fallen" women, backed by money from Angela Coutts, heiress of the Coutts banking fortune. The women who lived there learned how to read and write – another echo perhaps of Dickens' Mercury – and were rehabilitated into society.

Bee: Age Point conjunct Jupiter

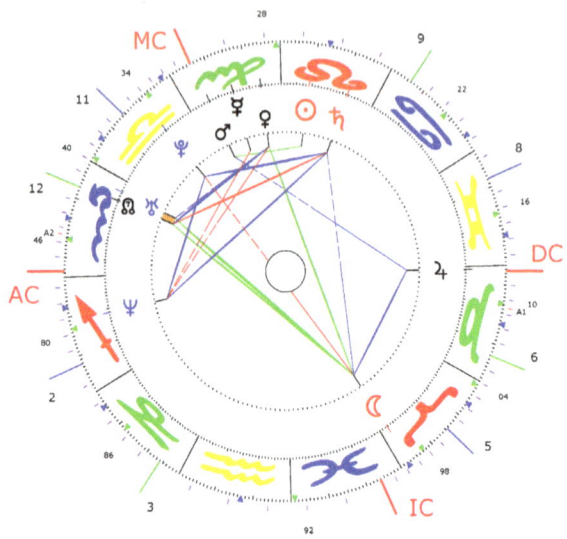

13.8.1976, 15:15, Nuneaton, England

Bee's Age Point is conjunct Jupiter, and recently crossed the DC when she was 36. At the DC there is a huge surge of energy which carries the individual from the lower, unconscious hemisphere of the chart into the upper hemisphere and the realm of consciousness. For many people the psychological effect of crossing the DC feels like the opening up of new horizons together with the opportunity to see life from a different viewpoint and perspective. Bee has a high-powered job in the legal profession, but she has recently given birth to her daughter and is learning and enjoying the new experience of motherhood. She married when her Age Point was on the Low Point of the 6th house. In the 6th house she had established her career and at the Low Point was ready to make the major decision of commitment to her marriage

She was pregnant the following year but had to have an emergency caesarian close to full term after her baby's movements had reduced. Bee's baby boy only lived for a few hours. Bee, supported by her husband, struggled to come to terms with this loss as her Age Point moved towards the end of Taurus and the 6th house. Life was heavy going, and although Bee became pregnant again, as her Age Point moved into the stress area before the DC she was understandably anxious and cautious. She took practical steps to ensure the health of her baby was safeguarded at every stage of her pregnancy.

Bee's daughter was born soon after her Age Point had crossed the DC, this coinciding with her psychological arrival in the upper, conscious hemisphere of the chart. The safe delivery of her baby daughter coincided with her Age Point conjunction to Jupiter. This birth has been welcomed by Bee with boundless joy and has brought a changed, expanded and sharpened perception of the world. The Hubers say that an Age Point aspect to Jupiter brings, "... an extension of consciousness and allows the wider connections between things to be seen… we are now conscious of our best qualities and can turn them to good account."

Bee describes this experience in her own words: "Regarding how I feel now my daughter has arrived, the predominant emotion immediately after the birth was overwhelming relief, which is not something I was expecting. I also felt that a great burden had been lifted from my life even though I had not appreciated that the burden was there in the first place. Though I have a great appreciation for the fragility of life and think about my baby boy every day we now have endless enjoyment and delight from our daughter, which is massively increased by the short time we had our son. In some respects I guess that my loss of my baby boy has opened my horizons and feelings beyond their previous boundaries."

Margaret Thatcher: Age Point conjunct Moon/Neptune

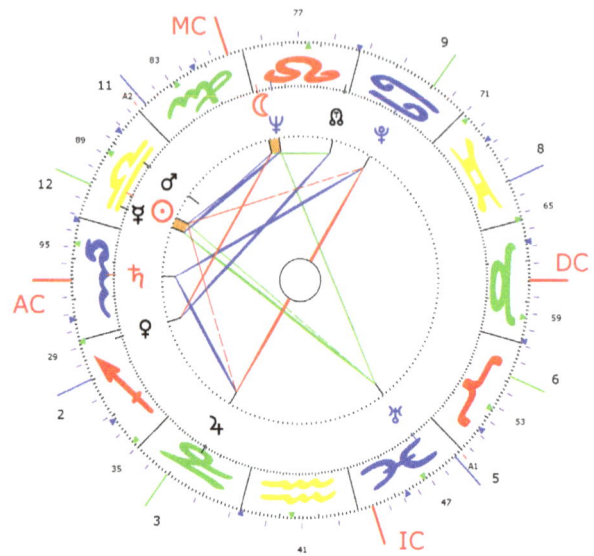

13.10.1925, 09:00, Grantham, England

The chart of former British prime minister Margaret Thatcher is dominated by a Projection figure. The focal, projecting planet is Uranus in the 4th house. It visually dominates the collective lower hemisphere of her chart and is indicative of her drive to make sweeping changes in British society and beyond whilst she was in power. In 1948, with her Age Point conjunct the focal projecting planet Uranus, Thatcher, as President of the Oxford University Conservative Association, attended her first Tory Party conference, representing the graduate branch of this association.

The planets forming the screen of the Projection figure are Sun/Mercury and Moon/Neptune. Both conjunctions were in evidence during the Thatcher years of power. The Sun/Mercury conjunction was expressed in her firm and forceful delivery once her voice had been lowered to create a more authoritative tone. Whilst Mercury is strongly placed in the cardinal zone of the 12th house, the Sun is stressed before the 12th cusp and would be expected to draw on the energies of all the other planets it aspects. Most notable could be its square to Pluto; she developed a tough and immobile stance, as evidenced during the Falkland's War in 1982 and the miners' strike in the 1984. Not for nothing was she known as The Iron Lady. A softer side, symbolised by the Moon/Neptune conjunction, was sometimes visible in her attention to image and her more feminine traits; she was fond of wearing hats when she was a government minister, and as prime minister she always wore pearls and was never seen without immaculately coiffed hair.

Thatcher's Moon is the highest planet in the whole chart. It is conjunct Neptune and is stressed before the MC. People with the Moon in this elevated position expect to be noticed and recognised. They feel important, often because the expectations put upon them as a child were very high. Thatcher's Age Point was conjunct Neptune in 1978 when, as leader of the Conservative Party, she was gaining prominence and recognition. In 1979 her Age Point was conjunct the Moon when the Conservative Party won the general election, and Thatcher became the UK's first woman prime minister. As she entered 10 Downing Street for the first time as prime minister, she quoted a paraphrased version of the Prayer of Saint Francis, almost certainly drawing on both Moon and Neptune at this time.

Age Point in Opposition

Oppositions also connect strongly with the energies of the planet they are opposing, but this encounter is different. It lacks the heightened intensity and immersion in the qualities of the planet concerned because the opposition is experienced at a distance. The energy of the opposition is held in tension and has a controlled, Saturnian quality. The Age Point certainly engages with the planet, but there is a sense of events happening to us from far away and of things being slightly out of our control. For the person who is reasonably self-aware there is no way they can side step an opposition from a planet; the experience and the psychological insights which go with it will have an impact on life and may bring subsequent changes in life orientation. But if the opposition is ignored, the theme that the planet represents will simply come back in a different form when the Age Point makes further aspects to it. The opposition can make us more defensive, so we may react by steadfastly ignoring what is going on in our lives. But if we are able to take on board what this aspect offers, and stay open to it, we will inevitably grow.

If the Age Point opposition to a planet occurs before the conjunction, the experience may be a more challenging. When we do arrive at conjunction with the same planet there is likely to be less apprehension as we will already be familiar with the qualities of the planet based on our previous Age Point experience of it.

Emile Zola: Age Point opposite Sun

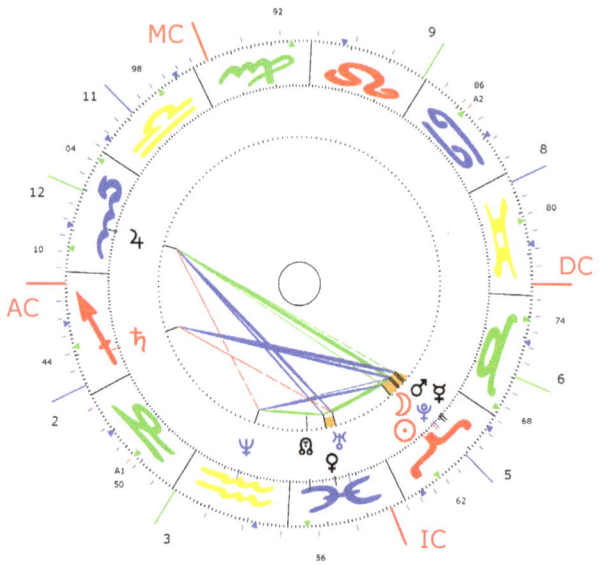

02.04.1840, 23:00, Paris, France

Emile Zola was a novelist and political journalist. His books were written in the style of literary naturalism of the late 19th century, and describe the realism of social conditioning, heredity and environment in the shaping of character. Zola was also a leading figure in the political liberalisation of France – maybe this is not too surprising for someone with five planets, including both Sun and Moon, in Aries.

When his Age Point was opposite Jupiter in 1871, the first of his twenty novels in the epic Rougon-Maquart series was published. This large and extensive body of work traced the natural and social history of a family living under the rule of the Second French Empire. The entire set of novels has over 300 characters and its scope has a Jupiterian quality. But it is the events that took place when his Age Point was opposite his Sun which stand out as being of great personal and psychological significance.

Any Age Point aspect to the Sun will shine a bright light upon that part of an individual which contains the core and essence of their personality. Zola's Aries Sun is strongly placed by sign, but is very close to the Low Point, suggesting that although he had a strong and urgent impetus to express his ideas and creativity, he may have had to rely on the presence of the other planets in the stellium to help with this. A

Low Point planet can shout to the rooftops, but unless it is trained and sensitively channelled, no-one will want to listen. With his Aries Moon tightly conjunct Pluto, it is not difficult to imagine how Zola might have felt intensely passionate about social and political issues. Both these planets, stressed before the 5th cusp, would rely on the energies of cuspal Mercury and Mars to get their message across. This was so in 1898 when Zola's Age Point was opposite his Sun. A leading French thinker of the time, Zola put his neck on the line and risked his career and reputation when the famous headline "J'accuse…" was published on the front page of the Paris newspaper L'Aurore. Zola spoke out in defence of army captain Alfred Dreyfus, in what became known as the Dreyfus Affair, and he wrote an open letter to the French president, in which he accused officials in the army of obstructing justice and of anti-semitism.

Dreyfus had been arrested and convicted of treason for revealing military secrets to the Germans, but the evidence was flimsy. Although there was a traitor somewhere within the ranks of the army, Dreyfus, a wealthy Jew, was used as a scapegoat and his court martial was full of dubious evidence. Dreyfus was convicted to life imprisonment and Zola took a stand against this injustice. Zola was tried and convicted of criminal libel and rather than go to jail he fled to England, but was allowed to return to France in time to see the government fall, and Dreyfus pardoned.

Roger: Age Point opposite Jupiter

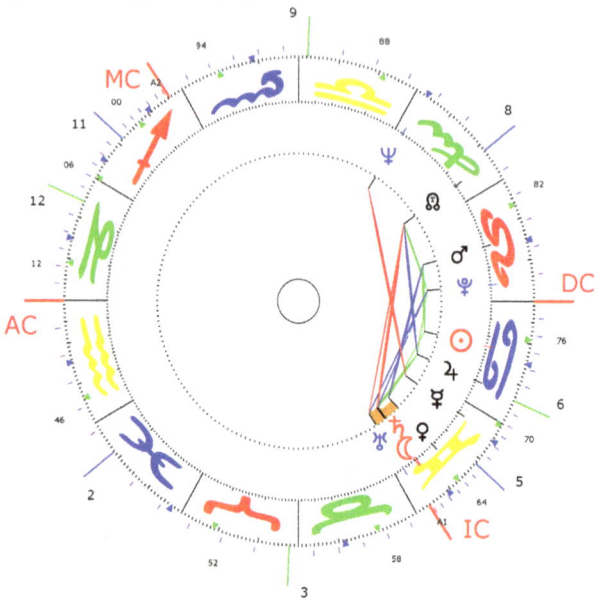

09.07.1942, 23:00, Lincoln, England

Roger's chart shows tightly packed planets on the "You" side, and close aspects connecting them. He retired at 64 from his career as a teacher as his Age Point entered the sign of Capricorn. With his Age Point in an earth sign, there was a marked change of orientation in his priorities as he became intensely practical, giving his home a complete makeover, undertaking much of the work himself.

In 2008, when his Age Point was opposite Jupiter, his first grandchild was old enough to attend nursery, allowing Roger's daughter – the child's mother – to return to work part time and resume her career. Life opened up for Roger in a new way as his horizons were expanded to include the responsibility of helping to bring up his grandson. He picked him up from nursery, cared for him and built up a lively and loving relationship with him. When the Age Point is opposite a planet we might feel we have less control over what is going on. Events and situations we find ourselves in can be challenging if we are not able to embrace them and go with the flow, but an opposition to a planet is easier to understand if the conjunction has already taken place. When Roger was 30 his Age Point was conjunct Jupiter in the 6th house and he was busy establishing his career as a teacher; at the opposition he was able to draw upon this experience of already being familiar with relating to and communicating with children.

Roger describes the period of time when his Age Point was opposite Jupiter as very positive, and as a wonderful opportunity to spend time with his grandson. He realised the importance of his influence as a grandparent and found the time they spent together enjoyable on many levels. Not only did it enable him to form a close bond with his grandson, it also helped and supported his daughter as she restarted her career. It's interesting to note that the Age Point was at the same time making a quincunx to his 4th house Gemini Moon which is in a tight conjunction with Saturn. Roger doesn't find it easy to articulate his feelings, but alongside the expansive influence of his Age Point opposite Jupiter he found he could open up and reconnect with his playful inner child through his interactions with his grandson.

Age Point in Semi-sextile Aspect

The semi-sextile, at 30 degrees, is the smallest aspect used in astrological psychology and is correspondingly the smallest aspect made by the Age Point. The semi-sextile has the inquisitive mercurial qualities of information gathering and fact finding, and its quality is like taking a small step forward on the path of learning. When the Age Point makes a semi-sextile aspect to a planet, it's as if there is a preliminary fact finding mission in progress. The qualities of the planet are introduced and touched upon, and information about it is gathered.

For example, a semi-sextile to Mars can stimulate us into gathering various snippets of information about what this planet represents in our lives for the duration of the Age Point contact. Bearing in mind that the energies and expression of the planet will be modified by the sign and house that it's in, our task of deepening our understanding of Mars in Aries will be quite a different task to the one we'd have if Mars was in Capricorn. Learning more about our Aries Mars, we might focus on how best to hone our leadership skills, and how to channel our initiatory impulses to best effect. With Mars in Capricorn we would be more likely to concentrate on the slow-burn approach, and with precision set out a long-term plan for the direction of our career.

Age Point in Sextile Aspect

The sextile aspect of 60 degrees has a very different flavour. It's more laid back and is focussed on finding harmony as it has Venusian qualities. When the Age Point makes a sextile aspect to a planet there is none of the busy, information-gathering as with the semi-sextile; in fact, the individual may be relatively unaware of the sextile transit of the Age Point. There may be an awakening of the need to bring more balance and harmony to bear on the expression of the planet being aspected, but if the sextile occurs whilst the Age Point is below the horizon and is still in the collective hemisphere of the chart, then this may not be recognised.

The sextile, in my experience, is more gentle and *laissez-faire*. There is not a lot of activity when the Age Point makes a sextile aspect to a planet, but more a stimulation of awareness of how the planet concerned could be expressed with greater poise and finesse. For example, a sextile to the Sun could put us in touch with not only how we regard ourselves, but with how we relate to others. Do we listen to them and acknowledge their viewpoints, or do we urgently push our own opinions on them? A sextile made by the Age Point to the Sun can have a beneficial effect in helping us understand how others see us, as well as invoking such questions as "What kind of person do I want to be or become?"

Age Point in Square Aspect

At 90 degrees, a square aspect made by the Age Point is one of the more powerful and challenging aspects in Age Progression. It is hard to ignore the square, even if we want to. Squares have a Martian quality and demand action. If we ignore the square and hope it will go away, it simply causes more trouble. The square has a lot of energy which seeks discharge through use and activity, so when the Age Point squares up to a planet in the chart, it's not exactly looking for a fight, but it will be looking for some action.

At the Age Point square to a planet the person might have a sense of having wrong-footed themselves. Things may not be going along as smoothly as before and mistakes can be made in response to what the environment is demanding and the challenges it's throwing up for us. Because the nature of the square is to work and take action, there will be a willingness on the part of the individual to set to and take on these challenges. The Age Point square is at the midpoint between the conjunction and the opposition, and in this position it can actively face up to the current demands as well as see the opportunities for growth that this situation offers. The Age Point square can bring change, and if we go along with that, and use the active energy of this aspect, we'll find that life will move on too.

Phoebe: Age Point square Sun/Mercury

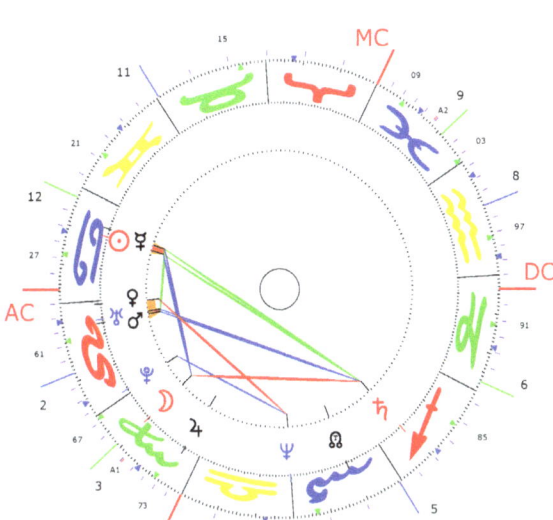

02.07.1957, 06:30, Bristol, England

Phoebe is a lively and dynamic woman in her mid-fifties. In her field of business she has won a prestigious Woman of the Year Award, and face to face she is very positive and engaging. She describes herself as a people person and knows her strength lies in working on the front line with others. At age 54, with her Age Point on the MC and making a trine aspect to Venus, she requested a consultation with me to help her clarify and focus on the changes in her life she was planning to make – namely to work part time so that she could put more into the charity care work she is involved in.

Twelve months on, whilst reviewing Phoebe's chart for her, I noted that her current Age Point in Aries and in 10th house was making a square to her 12th house Sun/Mercury. I wondered how her plans for scaling down her work commitments had progressed, asking if – as cardinal go-ahead Aries is an intercepted sign in her chart – she was feeling frustrated or thwarted in any way in her proposed life changes. I also wondered if there was some conflict between wanting to step back from the front line at work and do more of her own thing, set alongside still having to be, career-wise, in the spotlight with her Age Point in 10th.

Phoebe's response was interesting. Rather than having been able to go ahead with the changes she wanted to make, events have conspired to keep her working full time. Describing this in her own words she says, "I can't slow down". However, Phoebe has taken a philosophical stance on this setback and says that after accepting the situation, she's just getting on with it. She's deferred making changes to her lifestyle and although she felt disappointed for a while about this, she now feels as if she's rolling with the current flow of events and is working with what is possible here and now, in the moment.

With her current Age Point making a square to her Sun/Mercury conjunction, which are part of the Search figure in her chart, I asked if any searching and exploration of new areas of interest were calling. Phoebe said that such things have been put on the back burner for now, yet admitted that she needs to find more quality and satisfaction in her life outside of her career. For this reason her visits to the gym and to her personal pilates trainer are proving to be very important for what she calls "real me" time, when she can truly relax. Alongside this she is making sure there is time to see friends and family, a focal point which will help nourish the needs of her Cancerian Sun.

Still considering the current Age Point square activating both her Sun and Mercury, I asked how she was being challenged both in her career and on a personal level. She said that many changes were taking place in her business and professional life where she was not only required to use her communicative skills, but also her ability to plan strategically. She implied that there was a lot of activity going on inside for her right now, and I suspect this ties in with the focus on using her drive to communicate. There are also challenges being raised about the kind of person she wants to become. With the Age Point focus on her Sun, this is to be expected.

Although Phoebe is not yet able to stand back from the front line in her career, she has become involved in a local campaign to stop the building of houses on a green field site in her village, and describes her input here as very energised and active. She feels very strongly about this; her Sun in Cancer is rising to the challenge of the Age Point square and is showing its mettle as she takes a stand on something which will affect her community and neighbourhood.

I pointed out to Phoebe that there will be a change of energy in two year's time, when the Age Point moves from fiery Aries into earthy Taurus. This could bring her the opportunity to slow down and consolidate the plans she has had to shelve for now. Phoebe agreed that in two years time she will have a clearer idea of where her business commitments are heading, and already has what she called "a two week stock take" of what direction she might take planned for the near future.

Author's Chart: Age Point square Uranus

19.09.1945, 02:30, Tadcaster, England

The Age Point squares a planet at the mid-point between making a conjunction and opposition to the same planet. If the conjunction comes first in this sequence, the individual will already have had a close encounter with the planet concerned and will deepen their understanding and appreciation of its energies at the square and opposition. But if the cycle begins with the opposition the experience can be quite different. Events will feel slightly out of our control and we may feel confused, as though we do not have a finger firmly on the pulse of the direction our life is taking. Experiences will be coloured by the qualities of the planet involved. As time moves on we meet up with this planet when the Age Point makes the significant square and conjunction aspects. We should, by then, have a more comfortable working relationship with it.

When looking for examples to illustrate the Age Point square, I realised that I'd experienced this latter sequence in my own chart. Uranus is strongly placed on the 11th cusp and is one of the pinning planets, along with Moon and Mercury, in the Dominant Learning triangle. This aspect pattern lives up its name in my life as learning is an ongoing theme. Uranus is the planet associated with astrology, and as I'm a teacher and practitioner of astrological psychology, many of my students have noted the significance of its 11th house cuspal position in my chart.

At age 24, with my Age Point in Sagittarius on the cusp of the 5th house, and opposite Uranus, I was working as a trained teacher with 7-11 year olds. I had a lot of innovative and creative ideas and energy which I attempted to incorporate into my teaching. I was in a very formal school, with a formal, "old school" headmaster who clearly didn't approve of some of the approaches I was using. I felt hemmed in, thwarted and frustrated, subsequently became depressed and didn't know what was happening to me. I left my teaching job, took some time out and found a new teaching post. It was the right one for me. The head of the school I moved to positively encouraged all the teaching staff to be creative and to share and express their talents in the classroom. In retrospect I can see how this Age Point opposition to Uranus was stimulating me to move on, make changes, open up, learn and grow, so that when my Age Point squared Uranus 22 years later I was able to confidently take on the challenge of being Principal of the Astrological Psychology Association in the UK.

The square to Uranus coincided with my Age Point, at age 46, being on the Low Point of the 8th house. This is frequently experienced as a time of major change in life direction and in my life this was no exception. My role changed from being a teacher to being head of a school. Rather than this being a classic Low Point experience of stepping back from the demands of the environment, it was a time of high activity for me and I took this on willingly, working with the active energy of the square as I learned how to run an organisation teaching astrology. I had often heard Louise Huber say that at the Low Point we are closer to the soul's purpose and my experience at this time seemed to reflect her words. I had to draw deeply on my own inner resources as I learned how to administrate, direct and coordinate the worldwide distance learning programmes offered. My teaching skills were put to good use in the workshops and seminars I gave, the innovative energies of Uranus combining with the astrological psychology I was now teaching.

I worked very hard during the period following the Age Point's square to Uranus and I enjoyed what I was doing as I was able to be inventive and use my imagination. I was teaching once again, but this time with adults, in my own way and in my own school. When I was 60 my Age Point, which had been in Gemini for almost two years, reached conjunction with Uranus and entered the 11th house. Finally coming eyeball to eyeball with Uranus, I decided to start writing about astrological psychology, drawing on my experience as a teacher and practitioner of astrological psychology and activating the Dominant Learning triangle once again.

Age Point in Trine Aspect

Following the output of energy demanded by the Age Point square to a planet, the trine is far more relaxed and laid back. Trines are a 120 degree aspect and have a Jupiterian quality, making them more easy-going and optimistic in nature. When the Age Point is making a trine to a planet there will be a greater sense of ease, to the extent that this Age Point transit can be overlooked and sometimes is hardly noticed at all. There may be a general sense of harmony and consolidation with the trine, and the person might simply feel good and benign towards others if they are expressing the planet being aspected. With the trine, though, there is always the danger of laziness and inactivity, so being aware of this will help offset any complacency and smugness which could creep in if the individual thinks there is nothing to be done.

For example, an Age Point trine to Venus could manifest as the person being satisfied and content with the way they conduct their relationships, and provided there are no problems all will go well. They may allow themselves to become too complacent and *laissez-faire* though, and not pick up on warning signals which say "something's gone wrong in our relationship". It's often easier to ignore such signals, both in interpersonal relationships and in ourselves, and sit tight and do nothing. But the more positive side of the trine can be brought into play as the person recognises that an easy-going life approach can lead nowhere when things change and move on.

Age Point in Quincunx Aspect

When the Age Point makes the 150 degrees quincunx aspect to a planet it can be a powerful experience. It demands attention, much as the square does, but the energy of the quincunx is entirely different because it's concerned with raising consciousness in the individual rather than with busy outer activity. The quincunx has a Saturnian quality, but it shows a more benevolent side of Saturn. It is not a force which blocks or imposes limitations, but is an energy which acts like a wise mentor and guide. Whereas the semi-sextile can be likened to a small, information gathering step on the path of learning, the quincunx is a giant step. The quincunx Age Point aspect often involves deep learning, increased self-awareness and acknowledgement of things spiritual. With the quincunx there are no easy or quick fixes. It is slow-burning and encourages determination and persistence in pursuit of long-distance goals.

Age Point quincunx Pluto

In a workshop featuring Pluto I encouraged students to share their experiences of this planet when the Age Point was contacting it by aspect in their charts. Pluto is the planet associated with profound life events and with change and transformation on both inner and outer levels. Pluto, on its highest level, symbolises the search for perfection in ourselves. Bruno Huber often said that Pluto, at its highest, fully awake level would be transformative rather than destructive, and that personal growth would be continuous and ongoing. Feedback from students who attended the Pluto workshop suggests that the Age Point quincunx to this planet brought them deep, insightful and transformative learning experiences which they were not always aware of at the time. Only in retrospect were they able to appreciate the significance of the events and the long term effect they'd had on their personal development.

Paula: Age Point quincunx Pluto

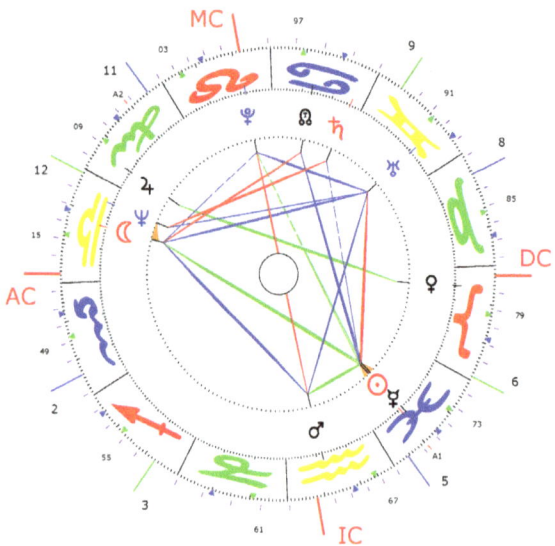

01.03.1945, 23:15 (22.15 GMT), 53.50 N, 002.37 W

Paula's chart contains a large fixed aspect structure resembling a kite, with a disconnected linear quincunx aspect pinned by Venus and Jupiter cutting across it. In itself, this aspect hints at the learning situations she could be confronted with, particularly in the realm of relationships as Venus is involved. However, it is the Age Point quincunx aspect to Pluto that Paula speaks of here. Pluto is strongly placed on the MC of her chart, making it the highest planet and one which the surrounding environment will pick up on and respond to. At the time the Age Point made a quincunx to Pluto, it was also conjunct her Sun/Mercury in Pisces in the 5th house, intensifying the impact of this event. Paula says:

"At this time I was 25 and had been married for about eighteen months to someone who was extremely jealous and possessive and physically violent towards me. I felt trapped and internally very angry, and about this time made the decision to leave and start again on my own. In spite of the circumstances it was a difficult decision as I had never lived alone, having been married from my parent's home. It was certainly a period of inner turmoil. In retrospect it was a deep learning experience. At the time of marrying I was still very angry inside from previous events – Mum dying just before my 21st birthday and Dad remarrying within twelve months – and I think perhaps I experienced externally what I was feeling internally."

Lorna: Age Point quincunx Pluto

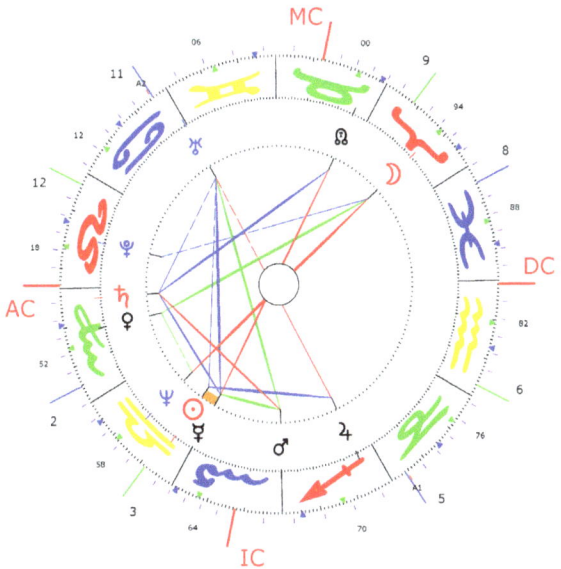

17.10.1948, 02:03, Liverpool, England

Lorna's chart is focussed on the "I" side and resembles a bird in a nest reaching out towards the 9th house with an open beak. Lorna admits that this area of the chart, concerned with higher learning, is something she aspires to, but she often doubts her ability to reach.

In the workshop on Pluto, Lorna shared her experiences of her Age Point approaching the quincunx to this planet at age 26, and there were marked similarities between her experiences and those of Paula.

The Age Point was below the horizon in the 5th house and the unconscious hemisphere of the chart. Lorna spoke of relationship problems with her husband, whose physical violence disrupted their marriage. They separated but got back together a year later when the Age Point quincunx to Pluto was exact. Lorna said she didn't learn the lessons life was giving her at this time, but did become interested in psychology, opening her up to looking more deeply into herself. She stayed with her husband until her Age Point was opposite Pluto, and was in the upper, conscious hemisphere of the chart. Then she finally left him.

When she was 41 and her Age Point was again making a quincunx to her 12th house Pluto, Lorna attended a week-long intensive course on psychology and counselling. She found this extremely challenging but it allowed her to learn more about herself and be open to insights which helped her transform from a rather quiet person who lacked confidence at the start of the week to someone who emerged as a changed woman. She was able to laugh again after all the tears she had shed left her washed clean and ready to face life with a new-found energy which came from deep within.

Margaret: Age Point quincunx Pluto

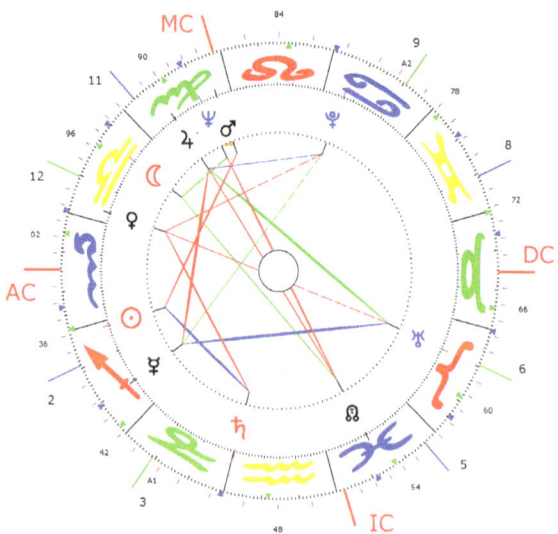

24.11.1932, 06:00 GMT, 52.11 N, 001.00 E

Margaret described her experiences of the Age Point making two quincunx aspects to Pluto, both before she had reached the age of 18. The first was in 1941, during World War 2 when she was 9. Her memories of this are quite hazy, and she says:

"It will not be easy to remember exactly my feelings and reactions at the relevant time, but here goes: I was evacuated to another part of England, which was quite an upheaval. I remember going to school along a very long lane and feeling very lonely. According to my mother I was very happy in my new surroundings and made many new friends."

Although Margaret struggled to recall the experience in any great detail, in the feedback she gave she did consider being evacuated and separated from her family as a significant experience; it "was quite an upheaval" perhaps says enough in the light of having no specific details. It is also interesting that her mother's perception of Margaret's experience is very different. Her mother said she made lots of friends, whereas Margaret's memory is of feeling very lonely at that time.

Margaret left school at age 14 and was working in a Building Society. Her Age Point opposed Pluto at this time, when she felt "very frightened and not very confident". She settled down into her new job out in the world and in 1949 experienced the second quincunx to Pluto, at age 17.

"This was not a happy time as my father, who I adored, had an affair and left home. He eventually returned but I can still remember the turmoil and lonely feeling."

Once again, the Age Point quincunx to Pluto is accompanied by feelings of loneliness, disruption and chaos. Margaret's subsequent life was not easy. She married twice, her first husband leaving her with two small children to raise, and her second husband bringing financial problems to their joint business venture and infidelity to their marriage. In spite of this, Margaret's feedback at the workshop ended on a positive note:

"Strange things have been happening. I no longer feel unable to cope, In fact, I feel I have come through it all a wiser person... I feel happy within myself and I enjoy life and have so much to be thankful for. Every day I feel is a bonus."

Transits and the Age Point

Age Progression is the primary method of timing used by astrologers trained in astrological psychology. My own experience suggests that Age Progression offers more than enough information, but I have also trained in more conventional astrological approaches which use transits as the primary method of timing. Although I rarely use transits, they can sometimes provide an additional supportive tool to use alongside Age Progression.

Although we do not primarily work with transits using the Huber Method, it is always worth noting if the Age Point is making an aspect to a planet when a transit to the same planet is taking place. If this is so, a "double whammy" effect may be experienced. The experience will be coloured by the house and the psychological life phase it's associated with and it can potentially be very powerful as it will be intensified by the planet concerned. The degree of intensity will be affected by the quality of the transiting planet. Common sense and astrological experience have to be brought into play to interpret and understand the possible effects.

Sue: Intense combined Transit and Age Point experience

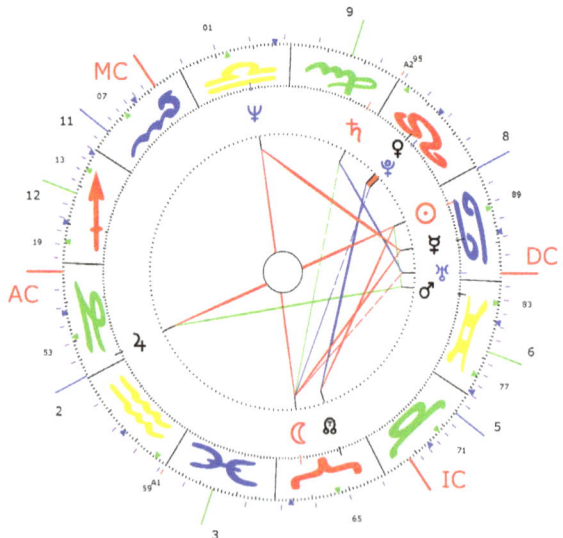

16.07.1949, 19:45, London, England

Sue is a professional astrologer who trained in astrological psychology with the Astrological Psychology Association. Whilst studying her own chart during training, she reconnected with an intense personal experience in 1970/71, when she was 21 and at university. Her Age Point was in Taurus in the 4th house, and had just travelled through the Low Point. It was square Venus and transiting Saturn was on the Age Point at the same time, also making a square to Venus.

Sue's 8th house Venus is conjunct Pluto, and in the period of time before both Age Point and transiting Saturn were on the same degree in the 4th house, they had both already squared Pluto. This was an intense time, and Sue describes it as a "combination of Venus as love, Pluto as transformation and Saturn as memory, guilt and pragmatism."

The focus of intensity was in the Spring of 1971 when Sue was unhappy with her lack of progress when working towards her finals at university. She arranged for a one-to-one discussion with a tutor whose methods she admired, and although she said little during their time together she found that he was able to tune in to the extreme tension that was preventing her from expanding mentally and developing intellectually. Sue was overjoyed because at last she felt that she was understood; she returned to her preparatory work for her finals with renewed energy.

She had a strong flashback memory of herself aged 4, capably and confidently drawing a picture. Memories of her childhood and the house where she lived came flooding back and as she reconnected with a life she had lost, she cried for several days, releasing a lot of tightly held emotion. Returning to her present situation, she realised that she had fallen in love with the tutor who had touched her inner core and who understood her. To be accepted, acknowledged and understood by another is a very powerful and healing experience. Sue knew that her feelings were inappropriate and apparently unreciprocated, but the experience of connection with her tutor, and the understanding he showed were instrumental in the process of self-discovery which had begun for her.

She also recalled a session she'd had with a clairvoyant two years previously, where the tutor had been described in graphic detail as "the right man, who would come" to help her lower her emotional defences and find her way once again. Sue says of this experience:

"So the dark night of the soul and its journey of love, pain and loss, represented by the Age Point square Venus/Pluto, encountered the practical manipulation of form and memory by a transit from Saturn that kept me in touch with reality, but at a price. The past was recaptured, transformed, and understood in a new light, the love for the man who opened the door was unreciprocated, but the stability of life was preserved and, undefeated, step by step, I knew I would find a way."

Part 5

Age Progression in the Moon Node Chart

The Moon Node Chart is unique to the Huber Method. It plays a significant role in the holistic approach used in astrological psychology, and it has its own Age Point which works alongside the Age Point in the natal chart. As a book on Age Progression would not be complete without mentioning this chart, a brief explanation of it is included here. However, the use of the Moon Node Chart is an additional refinement, and its interpretation is an advanced technique which is taught in the Diploma Course in Astrological Psychology offered by the Astrological Psychology Association. Whilst this chart with its own Age Point can offer additional information, it is recommended that the reader remains, for now, focussed on the Age Point techniques in the natal chart as described in this book. Understanding and using the Age Point in the Moon Node Chart is an advanced technique which, with experience, the reader may wish to pursue in greater depth at a later date.

Psychological meaning of the Moon Node Chart

The Moon Node Chart can be likened to a mirror. We can look into it to discover more about the shadow side of the personality. It can offer insights into those things which might be repressed and those things which we don't like in ourselves, and it can also give information about the accumulated knowledge and life experience we bring with us to this lifetime.

Author's Moon Node and Natal Charts

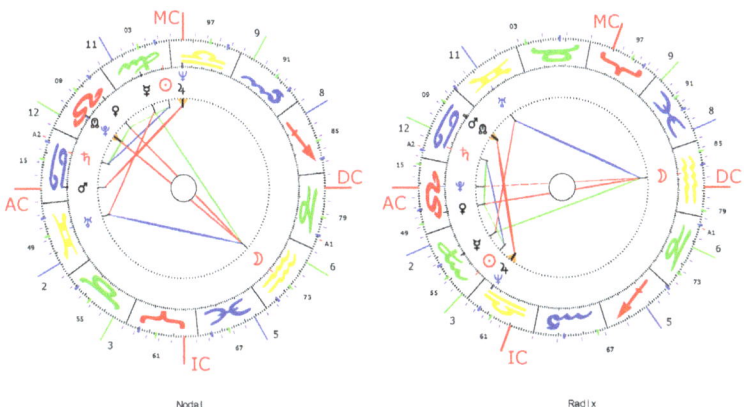

The Author's Moon Node and Natal Charts

I use my own natal and Moon Node Charts as an example to show how the Moon Node Chart reflects the aspect patterns and shaping shown in the natal chart. You will notice how the orientation of the aspect structure is different. In my Moon Node Chart it has a more vertical direction, whereas in my natal chart it's more focussed on the horizontal. This change of direction and orientation is just one of the significant features that should be considered. The Moon Node Chart signifies where we are coming from and the natal chart where we are now. A change in the overall aspect structure from a vertical to a horizontal direction suggests I might revert to the more vertical, individualistic motivation in life as shown in the Moon Node Chart, whereas what's important now is to align my motivation with the horizontal direction shown in my natal chart, which involves focussing on others as well as on my own individuality. Also note that the positions of the planets in these two charts are reversed, giving the mirror image effect, which makes looking at the Moon Node Chart rather like looking into a mirror, where what is seen is a reflection of the natal chart.

The Moon Node Chart is always used alongside the natal chart and never on its own. The two are designed to be used together, and this particular technique of using the two charts was researched extensively by Bruno Huber. The Moon Node Chart can offer insights, for those who are on a path of self-growth and awareness, into where they might be coming from. It can also highlight some of their more habitual patterns of response to everyday life, like the well-used behaviour patterns which are fallen into so easily and often unconsciously. The beauty of understanding and working with this chart is that it can help us to see what is going on in ourselves, decide if we want to keep things as they are or make changes, and then actively and consciously choose to leave our familiar and habitual patterns of response and behaviour behind us and move on.

Louise Huber says that when we look into the Moon Node Chart, we have to be completely harmless. This is important and should always be borne in mind when working with this chart. It has to be used with clarity and respect, and in a non-judgemental way.

Age Progression in the Moon Node Chart

When the Moon Node Chart Age Point is progressed, shadow qualities from this chart can be observed coming to light in everyday life. Behaviour which has not previously been recognised or acknowledged may emerge along with behaviour patterns which follow well-worn circuits.

Age Progression in this chart is traced anti-clockwise from the AC, as in the natal chart. It is measured at 5 degrees per year in each house. Each house covers 30 degrees and represents a time span of 6 years. The Age Point conjunct or opposite a planet in the Moon Node Chart will bring shadow qualities and behaviour to light. When this happens it could create problems for the individual; crises may occur when what has formerly been repressed comes into consciousness. It is sometimes found that a significant Age Point feature in the natal chart can be reflected in the Moon Node Chart, emphasising the whole experience of the person during that life phase. However, it should be borne in mind that when all the techniques concerning Age Progression are used and applied to the natal chart, there is usually more than enough information to draw upon.

The Age Point in the Moon Node Chart is covered in my book *The Living Birth Chart* together with example charts and the experiences of real people. Additional and detailed information on the Moon Node Chart can be found *Moon Node Astrology* by Bruno and Louise Huber.

Part 6

Chart Interpretations – Age Progression at Work

In this final section you will find a selection of chart interpretations using the charts of both well-known and ordinary people. These latter are the clients, friends and fellow astrologers who have agreed to their charts and life stories being used as examples of astrological psychology at work. Their accounts of Age Point experiences at different stages of their lives are a gift to you, the reader, on your own journey of learning, and I hope they will encourage you to test out Age Progression for yourself, using your own chart and life experiences.

    Interpretations of the charts of well-known people can make interesting reading too, but these interpretations are mine, based on my understanding and experience of using astrological psychology, and are not first hand accounts. When looking at the Age Point in these charts, I've referred to biographies and accounts of the lives and achievements of the person concerned, combining these with what I can see in the chart. There are plenty of significant correlations between Age Progression and life events in the charts of the well-known people I've chosen. Based on my own experience of working with Age Progression, I am confident that I've been able to understand and convey to you something of the essence of their experience.

    In these interpretations you will find references to aspect patterns together with other features of the Huber Method. All of these are covered in depth in my co-authored book *The Cosmic Egg Timer* and in my other books, *The Living Birth Chart* and *Aspect Patterns in Colour*. In addition to these, all the books written by Bruno and Louise Huber offer extensive and detailed information on all aspects of their work, as do the Astrological Psychology Association's courses.

The first sample interpretation I've chosen is of the chart of Berthe Morisot, one of the group of French Impressionist painters. Her chart offers many illustrative examples of the Age Progression techniques covered in this book.

Berthe Morisot: A Woman in a Man's World

Asked to name some of the Impressionist painters of the 19th century, most people would probably first come up with the names of Monet and Manet, and maybe Renoir or Degas. Far fewer, perhaps, would remember the name of Berthe Morisot. As a group of artists, the Impressionists were probably the most abused and reviled artists of their time and it would have seemed highly unlikely that a woman would join them. Yet Berthe Morisot did. She joined the group and stayed with them through good times and bad, and she held her own amongst them as an equal and an artist in her own right.

Berthe Morisot

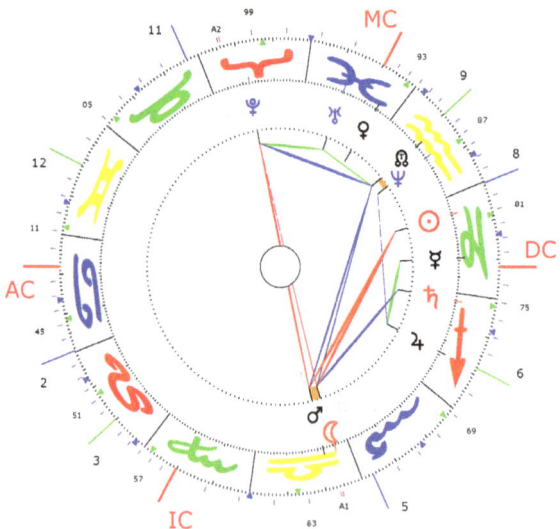

14.01.1841, 15:00, Bourges, France (RRAA)

Berthe Morisot was born in Bourges, France, into an upper middle class family. Her father was administrative head of the Cher department, of which Bourges is the capital. She was brought up in considerable comfort and throughout her life never had any financial worries. It is debatable whether a woman artist with lesser means would have survived and been successful without the backing of family wealth. But it was not money alone that supported Morisot; she came from a loving, caring family who encouraged both Berthe and her sister Edma in the expression of their artistic potential.

An initial look at Berthe's chart shows a striking, vertical aspect structure confined almost exclusively to the DC hemisphere, with a fairly even distribution of planets spanning the 4th to 10th house. What does this tell us about Berthe as a person? It certainly suggests that interacting with others is likely to have been important for her, and the focus of her output would have been through the tenanted houses on that side of her chart. But within the context of the very vertical chart structure, she would have sought to assert herself as an individual in her own right. And although she may not have consciously set out to do so, she did gain recognition and acclaim in her chosen field as an artist.

The colour ratio of red/green/blue aspects in her chart shows a slight lack of red when set alongside the number of blue and green aspects. When blue/green dominates this indicates heightened imagination and sensitivity. Berthe and Edma both showed artistic talents early on, and some biographers claim that they were related to the Rococo artist Fragonard. Berthe's mother encouraged their budding artistic inclinations, and arranged for the sisters to have painting lessons when the family moved to Passy, near Paris, in 1855.

Unaspected Venus

When Berthe was 16 her Age Point was opposite unaspected Venus in Pisces. An unaspected planet can be a blessing or a bind. It depends on how it is used and activated by the individual. Unaspected planets have the ability to range far and wide in the environment, seeking out what attracts them according to their inherent qualities. Venus in Pisces, and unaspected in the chart of a painter, suggests an attraction to what is harmonious and beautiful in the surrounding world. The unaspected nature of the planet would encourage an open eyed approach to take in all that was seen. Although Venus is unaspected it sits close to the Ear/Eye aspect pattern at the top of Berthe's chart, looking like a detached observer or onlooker. It's almost as if Venus was waiting to be called upon, to be activated and pulled fully into the overall aspect structure of the chart where there was clearly an imaginative talent at work. When the observations and experiences of an unaspected planet are brought back and fed into the whole chart they can enrich the scope and potential of the individual concerned. If this does not happen, the planet will behave like an ungrounded distractor, flipping this way and that, responding to new things as they come along but never quite integrating them. Berthe's unaspected

Venus didn't behave in this way because what was observed and experienced was then embraced and integrated into her work.

The Ear/Eye

Berthe's Ear/Eye, also called an Information triangle, dominates the top of the chart. Composed of two green semi-sextiles and one blue sextile it both looks and acts like a tiny radar dish. This aspect pattern is highly sensitive to picking up and 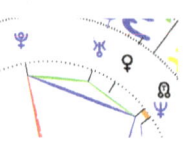 storing all manner of information from the surrounding environment. It can gather this effortlessly and keep it in reserve for future use. Information, visual and sensory impressions are absorbed by the green semi-sextiles, and then stored in the blue sextile, awaiting access when the need arises. The pinning planets in the Ear/Eye are significant and in Berthe's chart all three transpersonal planets and the Moon's Node are involved. Uranus is at the apex, and is the outlet for what has been absorbed and stored away. In Berthe's chart Uranus sits alongside unaspected Venus, both of them high in the chart.

Uranus is concerned with evolution and with finding the perfect world. Expressed at its highest level, it is about connecting with the pure creativity of the universe. In Berthe's chart Uranus is in Pisces in the 10th house, perhaps helping to expand this drive even further on a personal level. Viewed in the historical context of the time, she was able to break new ground as a woman and a painter. As a woman, her subject matter has a soft, feminine flavour – portraits of women with children, everyday domestic scenes, landscapes and flowery corners of gardens. At the time, women painters were expected to only paint indoor, domestic scenes and Berthe did this with great sensitivity. But she also extended her range to paint out of doors, in nature, something which it was not expected, or even approved of, for a woman. Even more remarkable is that she became the only woman artist in a group of men, all of them breaking boundaries in the style of painting they were experimenting with and pursuing. The Impressionists were initially considered by the art critics of the time to be too revolutionary, not only in their choice of subjects, but in the way they applied the paint. But Berthe chose to join them and stay with them.

Age Point opposite Uranus

In 1860, when she was 19 and her Age Point was in the 4th house and opposite Uranus, she grew tired of dutifully copying the paintings of Old Masters at the Louvre, as directed by her then teacher, Guichard. At the time it was deemed inappropriate for young ladies to paint anywhere else but indoors. Berthe, with her strongly placed Uranus, wanted to find her own way and suggested that she should start painting out of doors. Guichard was shocked, telling her mother that there was a danger of Berthe becoming too passionately involved in painting. It may have been that he considered professional male painters unsuitable company for a genteel young lady, or that she might have been unprepared for the harsh criticisms and rejections that were part of a professional painter's life. But he knew nothing of the strength of Berthe's Uranus. In 1861 she found the teacher she needed in Camille Corot, who had become an established master in the 1850s but who did not normally accept pupils. He allowed Berthe and Edma to study with him and to work *en plein air* – in the open air – where they learned to paint from life. When she found the teacher she needed, Berthe's Age Point was making an active, square aspect to Saturn. This planet, at its highest level of expression, can act as a wise guide and mentor, and Corot entered her life in this role.

The Paris Salon

Berthe's life took on a new dimension. She met and mixed with successful painters, took up sculpture and in 1864, when her Age Point was conjunct Moon/Mars and opposite Pluto, she had her first landscape canvases accepted for exhibition by the Paris Salon. She was 23 at the time, and continued to exhibit at the Salon for many years to come. It was a significant event in the context of her Age Progression too. The conjunction with Moon/Mars marked the first direct contact made with a planet and with the overall aspect structure of her chart. Up until this time, her Age Point had been moving, from birth, through a completely empty area of the chart. People who experience this describe it as like swimming for the shore but never quite getting there. Berthe's experience could have been similar. She had been working at developing her painting, she had asserted her desire to paint en plein air and she had learned how to transfer what she saw in real life on to her canvases. With this conjunction, it could have felt to Berthe that at last, she had arrived.

Intercepted signs

At the same time, when she made this first direct contact with these planets, she may also have realised that there was so much more potential to be tapped into and so much more of life to be lived. Moon/Mars and Pluto, which they oppose, are in the intercepted signs of Libra and Aries. The expression of intercepted planets is always more challenging as they occupy signs with no house cusps, which provide pathways out into the environment. Being intercepted, they draw on the energy of the other non-intercepted planets they are in aspect to, using these as a conduit for their expression. In Berthe's case, Moon/Mars would seek expression via her Capricorn Sun, 6th house Saturn and Neptune conjunct the Moon's Node, whereas Pluto would look to Uranus, Neptune and the Node. This in turn would awaken and activate the blue/green Ear/Eye aspect pattern which I've speculated upon as being very important in her chart.

In 1868, with her Age Point moving through Scorpio and the 5th house of relationships, and making a sextile aspect to her Sun, she was introduced to Edouard Manet by fellow painter Fantin-Latour. They met at the Louvre and became good friends. Berthe persuaded Manet to try *plein air* painting, which she had been doing since becoming Corot's pupil. She became one of Manet's favourite models and he painted her portrait several times. Age Point aspects to the Sun always bring a heightened sense of self, and as Berthe's relationship with Manet was as an equal rather than a pupil, her confidence and awareness of her own creativity and abilities is likely to have received positive reinforcement at this time.

Sign changes

As her Age Point moved through houses 5 and 6, it changed signs from Scorpio to Sagittarius, and was conjunct first Jupiter then Saturn. How might this have affected Berthe's career in a personal and professional way? A change of sign is always significant as there is a change in orientation and energy, based on the element and qualities of the new sign the Age Point moves into. Berthe's Age Point was in practical earthy Virgo when she was having formal lessons with Guichard; when it moved into Libra, Corot agreed to take her and Edma on as pupils so they could widen their subject matter and learn to paint from life in the open air. This would have heralded an opening up to the world of nature, where her perception of outdoor light and shade, and how these related to people and natural objects would have made a big impression. I imagine that her unaspected Venus would have revelled in this. She is quoted as saying, "It is important to express oneself... provided the feelings are real and are taken from your own experience."

As the Age Point moved into fiery and optimistic Sagittarius, Edma married and decided to give up painting. Berthe continued to paint alone, using Edma and her children as models in some of her subsequent paintings. Going it alone must have brought an element of adventure into her life as it marked the start of something completely new and exciting for Berthe. Over the next few years she was to encounter, by conjunction, Jupiter, Saturn and Sun.

Conjunct Jupiter, Saturn and Sun

Jupiter in its natural sign of Sagittarius speaks of expansion and risk, together with opportunities to gain wisdom by real life experience along the way. With her Age Point conjunct Jupiter in 1870, Berthe exhibited two paintings at the Salon. One was praised enthusiastically by Manet, so she presented it to him as a gift. The other she was not so sure about, and when she mentioned this to Manet, he offered to retouch it. But when she saw what he'd done, Berthe was confronted by a personal dilemma. Her painting was like a caricature of its former self. She was torn between withdrawing it and offending Manet, or risking ridicule by showing it. She showed it, and was relieved that it attracted little attention. Although there is no way of verifying this via Berthe's first hand experience, the episode does indicate the potentially risky, impetuous nature of direct contact with Jupiter in its own sign, along with learning from first hand experience of what is, and what is not, wise! This Jupiterian experience would undoubtedly have been fed back into the Ear/Eye via the linear aspect to the Moon's Node and Neptune.

In 1874, her career became more established. With her Age Point conjunct Saturn that year she exhibited, as the sole woman, in the first Impressionist exhibition in Paris. She also married Eugene, brother of her friend Edouard Manet whilst her Age Point was not only conjunct Saturn, but was also making aspects to her Sun and Moon, drawing in all three ego planets (Sun, Moon, Saturn) at this significant juncture of career and personal life. From then on, Berthe was very publicly a part of the Impressionist group who exhibited regularly in Paris, and then had shows in London and New York. Notably, Berthe's Age Point was conjunct her Sun at the time of one of the Paris exhibitions, where her work was hailed by critics as one of the Impressionist movement's outstanding exponents, and her pastel colour palette highly praised.

Berthe gave birth to her daughter, Julie, in 1878. She and Julie became very close, Julie becoming her favourite model who she painted many times. Berthe continued to exhibit, and became a significant member of the Impressionist group and movement, organising and financing shows of their work. Her husband Eugene Manet died in 1892, just a few months before the opening of her first and only one-woman exhibition, and as her Age Point was changing signs from Aquarius to Pisces. Berthe died suddenly in 1895, aged 54, from a lung infection contracted whilst nursing Julie. Was there some significance in this? Her Age Point was close to the midpoint between Venus and Uranus who sit like sentinels on either side of the MC, and who had both been significant players in her life as an artist.

Berthe is quoted as saying, "My ambition is limited to capturing something transient". The influence of Venus and of her own femininity underlie the lightness of touch and the softness of colour in the portraits and landscapes she painted. The quality of light in many of them is transient and has an ethereal feel. She also said, "A love of nature is a consolation against failure" and it is suggested that she often lacked confidence in her ability as a painter. Yet she made her mark, a creative woman in a man's world, at a time when women were not expected or encouraged to shine beyond the confines of the drawing room. The vertical direction of her aspect structure, together with her 10th house Uranus at the apex of the Ear/Eye adds the edge which made it possible for her to succeed as a woman and a member of a group of reviled artists.

* * * *

Fred Astaire: "Can't act. Slightly bald. Also dances."

I'm a dancer, and I started dancing when I was four years old. I revelled in learning the skills and movements in this new-found activity and I loved all the sparkly costumes and make up that went on for performances. It's not, then, altogether surprising that I began dancing when my Age Point was conjunct Venus in Leo in the 1st house of my chart. I still dance now, for enjoyment rather than performance, and there is one iconic dancer who I never tire of watching. That is Fred Astaire, whose impeccable technique, style and performance is immortalised in the films he made in the 1930s and 1940s.

Bruno Huber, originator of the Huber Method of Astrological Psychology, spoke of Pluto as offering the ideal of a "perfect being", of someone who has perfected the personality through an evolutionary process, always holding the desired goal of perfection in mind. In lectures and seminars, he described this as being akin to the hero's journey, where transformations are made en route to the goal of the perfection being sought. He encouraged students to cultivate an image for themselves of the perfect being by having their own heroes and heroines, people whose qualities and attributes they admired and aspired to. In their book *The Planets and their Psychological Meaning* the Hubers say, "Pluto contains a model that tells us what this perfection must look like". Fred Astaire, as we will see, was constantly seeking perfection in his dancing.

Fred Astaire

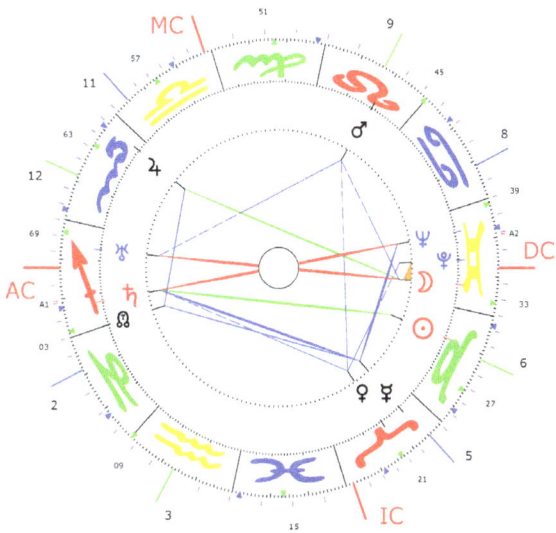

10.05.1899, 21:16, Omaha, Nebraska, USA

Astaire was born Frederick Austerlitz, the son of an American born mother and an Austrian father. His chart reminds me of a see-saw or swing boat seeking to achieve balance; it's not quite there but it's not far off either. I also see what could be a Kite configuration spanning the horizontal axis of the chart, but it's not complete and gives the impression that everything is still docking into the right position to complete this figure, and once again, it's not quite there yet. One significant thing that Astaire was renowned for was his never-ending quest for perfectionism in his choreography and dance routines.

The aspect structure, on initial inspection, appears to be composed of quadrangular figures, but a closer and more detailed look reveals that this is an illusion as there are interlocked triangular figures along with several linear aspects. The shaping of the overall aspect structure gives information about the person's inner motivation and what drives them; Astaire's looks quadrangular, which would make him Fixed/security-oriented, but in fact there is a mixture of Mutable (triangular) figures and Cardinal (linear) aspects. This indicates a flexible and fluid approach to life, of being able to move on with changes and go with the flow. But at the same time there is an underlying push of restlessness and determination which comes from the cardinality of the linear aspects.

The direction of the aspect structure is horizontal, with the rickety and still incomplete Kite flying towards the "You" side. This is emphasised by the Moon/Pluto conjunction straddling the DC and the presence of Neptune in the 7th house. In spite of his Sagittarian ascendant, with planets in this sign adding emphasis, it is often planets on or around the DC which are picked up first and foremost by the environment as these are what others first encounter. Moon in Gemini is easy to see in Astaire's slim and lightweight frame and his smoothly shaven face. His looks were quirky and unconventional, but his charm and pulling power are undeniable; a combination of Moon conjunct Pluto and opposite Uranus, with the 7th house Neptune standing nearby like an overseer. After a Hollywood screen test, producer David Selznick wrote of Astaire "I am uncertain about the man, but I feel, in spite of his enormous ears and bad chin line, that his charm is so tremendous that it comes through even on this wretched test"!

The rickety Kite and the need for perfection

Astaire's Kite is incomplete and in most instances I would decline to "see" a nearly-complete aspect pattern where one does not exist, sticking with what is already there and working with that. However, the near-Kite kept drawing my attention. Incomplete aspect patterns can indicate a lot of energy being expended by the individual to complete the pattern themselves. There is a striving towards bridging the gaps that are there and in bringing the pattern into a cohesive whole. The person may sense that there is something as yet incomplete within themselves and seek to resolve this by trying always to excel as completion of the pattern – and perfection – is sought. More on this later.

The Kite aspect pattern, when complete, is composed of a Small Talent triangle at the top with a Large Talent triangle underneath. Together they form a large quadrangular figure with a central strut, the opposition, running through the middle. However, the other component parts of this figure are the two Ambivalence figures which lie on either side and in different areas of the chart. These can give

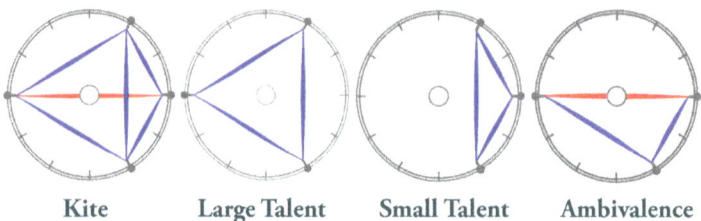

Kite   Large Talent   Small Talent   Ambivalence

rise to either/or behaviour: the person is either completely engrossed in an issue or activity, or he avoids it. If the preoccupation is total, the person can harness the potential talent in the small triangle, then develop and express it.

In Astaire's rickety and not-quite-complete Kite, the Small Talent triangle is mostly complete. Only the crossed over sextiles to the Moon/ Pluto conjunction at the apex make it not quite come together. It is this triangle in the Kite which indicates an artistic ability or gift which can be developed, the pinning planets offering information on the nature of the talent and how it might be expressed. The inclusion of Venus and Mars in this pattern suggests a certain glamour, charm and allure coupled with taste and a touch of class together with the capacity to present this to the world in a conspicuous way. Astaire's Mars in Leo is strong by sign at 11 degrees and strong by house as it's cuspal. It is the highest planet in the chart and expressed at its highest level, Mars is generally recognised as signifying the accomplishment and practice of specific skills.

The Large Talent triangle, at the tail end of this incomplete Kite, is itself incomplete and more open and porous, meaning that the energy will drain away here through the gap in the aspect structure between Saturn and Uranus. The Hubers, in *Aspect Pattern Astrology*, say that the planet or planets at the tail end of the Kite usually indicate the task to be accomplished in this figure, with the other three planets in the Kite working towards its development. Both Saturn and Uranus are interestingly placed at the not-quite-tail-end of the Kite. 12th house Uranus is stressed before the ascendant and psychologically much more attuned in 1st house matters whilst Saturn is optimally placed on the Balance Point in the 1st house indicating that all matters pertaining to the physical can be accomplished with poise and comparative ease. But Saturn could also prove a hard task-master in Astaire's quest for perfection. Both planets straddle the AC and the energy leak is here, in this area of the ascendant, the very place where we nurture our own self-image and aspire to be as perfect (in our own eyes) as we can be. The Hubers say of people with a Kite that they "strive for perfection, not necessarily because they want to reach a fixed state though, but to be true to themselves, i.e. in all situations to act in line with their innermost convictions and their heart of hearts."

Astaire the Perfectionist

I would normally have not focussed too much on the rickety and incomplete Kite in Astaire's chart, but having started researching details of his life and career, I discovered that he was indeed constantly striving for perfection and, perhaps, to complete this incomplete figure, spurred on by stickler Saturn on the Balance Point in the 1st house.

Ginger Rogers, his most famous on-screen dance partner, described Astaire's uncompromising high standards: "Sometimes he'll think of a new line of dialogue or a new angle for the story… they never know what time of night he'll call up and start ranting enthusiastically about a fresh idea… No loafing on the job on an Astaire picture, and no cutting corners." He is reputed to have insisted on numerous rehearsals and retakes in order to conserve costs (Saturn again?) for the actual shooting of a dance number. With so much preparation, the shooting inevitably went well, but Astaire agonised during the whole process, frequently asking colleagues for acceptance of his work. Director Vincente Minelli said of him, "He always thinks he is no good", and Astaire said of himself, "I've never yet got anything 100% right. Still, it's never as bad as I think it is." No, it was not. A friend who has trained as a teacher of the Alexander Technique tells me that Astaire's dancing is held up as an example of the kind of ease of motion that can be achieved by using just what strength and effort are required, but no more.

Astaire's Age Progression
Astaire's Age Progression highlights some significant life events too. Using his chart as a life clock, and applying some of the techniques outlined in this book, several meaningful events are pinpointed. The conjunction and opposition of the Age Point with a planet prove the most powerful and it is interesting to see how the conjunctions to Sun, Moon, Pluto and Neptune coincide with key events in Astaire's career. At age 31, with his Age Point just into the 6th house and conjunct his Taurean Sun, his tap dancing was recognised as among the best. Robert Benchley, the American humourist and columnist wrote, "I don't think I will plunge the nation into war by stating that Fred is the greatest tap dancer in the world." The Age Point crosses the DC at 36 years, and with a cluster of planets around this point in Astaire's chart, it's not surprising that this period of his life was full of significant events. At this time, too, the crossing of the Age Point over the DC and its entry into the upper, conscious hemisphere of the chart is often experienced as a time when the individual comes into their own and feels more empowered to take on new directions in life. When his Age Point was conjunct the Moon at age 35, Astaire starred in the film *Gay Divorcee* which was ground breaking in that it ushered in a new era in filmed dance. At age 36-37, when his Age Point was conjunct Pluto, he was involved in making the films he is best known by, with Ginger Rogers as his partner. He not only performed, but

choreographed the dance routines, once again applying his unrelenting perfectionist touch to all he worked with. His partnership with Rogers raised them both up to star status, bringing some light relief and offering a distraction, via the silver screen, from the hard times of the thirties and the darkening days of impending war. Actress Katherine Hepburn is reported to have said of the Astaire/Rogers partnership, "He gives her class and she gives him sex." I'm assuming she meant sex appeal here but this quote brings a smile to my face as it was made during the period his Age Point was conjunct Pluto.

When the Age Point reached its conjunction with Neptune, Astaire appropriately became more involved with camera and filming techniques. He introduced innovative ideas for filming dance, and insisted that the camera should be stationary and the dance should be filmed in a single shot, holding the dancers in full view the whole time. He also insisted that all the song and dance routines be integrated into the plotlines of the film; the dance was used to move the plot along. Whilst the Age Point was conjunct Neptune, it was also opposite Saturn, his everlasting task-master on the journey to perfection. At this time he applied it to the actual filming techniques.

Astaire supposedly retired from dancing in 1946 and founded the *Fred Astaire Dance Studios* in 1947 when he was 48, with his Age Point conjunct Mars on the 9th cusp. However, he did the famous "comeback" that many movie stars of that era seemed to, and went on to make several musicals throughout the 1950's. He eventually went on to develop his acting career, receiving rave reviews in the 1959 nuclear war drama *On the Beach*. This coincided with his Age Point opposite Mercury and on the 11th cusp at age 60.

Saturn at its highest level, where it acts as a wise guide and mentor, promoting deep learning, has the last laugh as far as the quest for perfection is concerned. At the age of 75, Astaire won a Golden Globe for Best Supporting Actor, and a BAFTA award, for his performance in *The Towering Inferno* as his Age Point made its second conjunction with this planet. Not bad for someone whose screen test report read "Can't act. Slightly bald. Also dances."

* * * *

Denise: Seeker and Teacher

Denise is one of the people who agreed to her chart and life experience, particularly in the context of Age Progression, being used in this book. She is an advanced student of astrological psychology, studying the material in depth and at Diploma level with the Astrological Psychology Association. She is undertaking this course of study primarily for her own interest and self-development, and has agreed to the use of her own words in this interpretation.

Denise

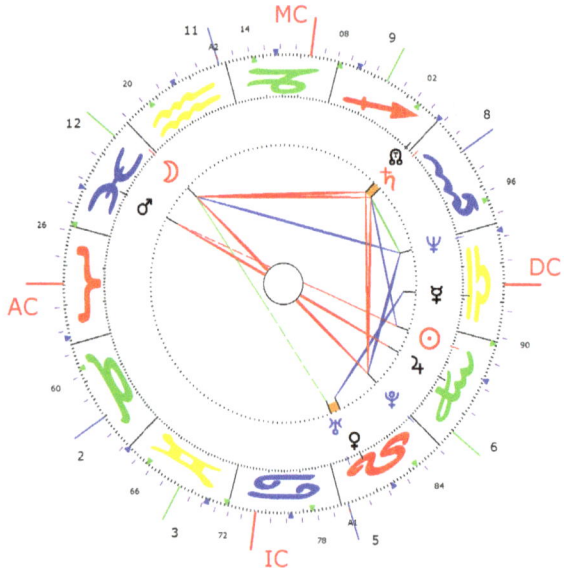

18.09.1956, 19:20, Saginaw, Michigan, USA

An initial look at Denise's chart reminds me of an energetic arrowhead very pointedly aiming its energy into the 8th house of the chart with Saturn and the Moon's Node at the tip. The all-red Achievement/ Efficiency triangle is the first thing that takes the eye… but wait a minute… this triangular aspect pattern might dominate visually, but it is a component part of a quadrangular aspect pattern in her chart with a fixed motivation. So rather than being motivated towards activity, flexibility and change with her triangular red arrowhead, she could be, deep down, more concerned with preserving and maintaining what is familiar and what she has worked hard to establish.

The large fixed aspect pattern of which the arrowhead is a part is known as an Animated figure and in addition to the Achievement/Efficiency triangle it contains two Small Learning triangles and an Ambivalence figure. Work, learning and energetic output may be sporadic, with a flip-flopping effect between active and passive modes. But experiential learning and the acquisition of new skills are very much a feature of this figure, and Denise is a person who has seemingly never tired of learning throughout her life, interspersing this with periods of consolidation.

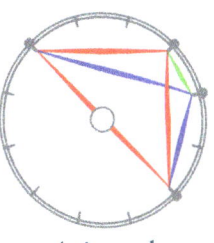

Animated

Empty houses

Denise, when exploring the significance of Age Progression in her chart, noted that the first four houses were empty. These cover the first quadrant of the chart and the first 18 years of life. Denise says: "Without the mediating influence of planets in the first four houses, I believe I experienced the influence of the signs more strongly than might otherwise have been the case. I guess I would say that the "empty" first quadrant at this time in my life served to intensify the feeling any child might have of external influences shaping circumstances and having no control over them oneself; it certainly did not mean that nothing of significance took place there. One significant event during this period was my first trip to Germany in 1964 with my parents and my brother, which came shortly after the Age Point in Taurus opposed my natal Saturn in Scorpio. We did a lot of travelling that visit so there were a lot of sensory impressions for a 7 year old to take in and some of them are quite vivid for me, but my strongest impression of that visit was meeting my "Omi", my Mom's stepmother, whom I adored from the moment we met."

Denise picks up on the Age Point moving through sensuous earthy Taurus at the time of this first visit, and recalls the sensory memories she has of this period as a 7 year old on her first visit to Europe, perhaps in the form of new smells, tastes and sounds. She also notes the significance of the Age Point opposite her 8th house Saturn at this time, and links it with meeting – and adoring – her step-grandmother who was to become an important figure and mentor in her life.

Whilst Denise's Age Point was still in the fixed 2nd house her family moved to Germany to live with Omi. This was a big step for her and she describes it here in the context of Age Progression: "During the summer of 1966, just after the Age Point transited Low Point 2, we moved to Germany. This was difficult for me, being uprooted and giving up many of our familiar possessions (2nd house), including selling our home. The saving grace for me was that we lived with my adored Omi in her house (a thin thread of stability for a Fixed House circumstance). Starting school in a foreign country was probably made even more difficult for a shy child coming as it did just after the Age Point was conjunct the Low Point of the 2nd house. My dad wasn't around much during this time, increasing a sense of insecurity, as he sought employment. When nothing suitable was found, he returned to the States ahead of us to return to his job and to purchase a home. The influence of Gemini in the 2nd house can certainly be seen as a big part of the experience – changing schools from the States to Germany, then schools and a new house yet again when we moved back to the States about 6 months after we left. Flexibility and adaptability were clearly demanded of me in the situation and were also in evidence in the state of flux for our family at that time. The mutability of my Sun sign Virgo together with the Age Point in the mutable zone of the 2nd house, and in the mutable sign of Gemini, were big factors for me."

I'd also suggest that alongside the influence of the Age Point in Gemini during this period, Denise's Animated figure played a part. The two Small Learning triangles in this figure would have been fully engaged as she had to learn not only a whole new culture, but a new language too, and the drive and energy embedded in the red aspects in this figure would have been an essential part of her own survival tactics in these new circumstances. The first quadrant is associated with surviving what life brings our way.

Time moved on, and Denise, now in her early twenties and back in the United States, graduated and began a new job in 1978 as her Age Point moved over the 4th house Low Point. At the same time, she met the man who was to become her first husband. Her Age Point was in the 4th house, and in the sign of Cancer, and in her own words, she describes this period of time as she experienced it: "We became engaged and, in spite of the strong doubts I had about this decision as the wedding drew near, we married in August of 1979 in a large, traditional wedding. In retrospect, I can see that the marriage to someone from my home town with many family connections and deep roots there was a sort of culmination of the unconscious collective influence on me and a way to hang onto the emotional (Cancer) aspects of something familiar and conventional, yet it was also a move away from my family – a way to perhaps bring the "safe" past (i.e. what was familiar) with me into a less certain future. What followed in this mutable zone of the 4th house was leaving my parents' home to establish a new one in a new city, a new job for me, beginning Graduate school at a large university; my husband lost his job and found a new one that required him to be on the road. So many changes were taking place, it seemed as though things were gearing up, drawing me into the activity, adventure and transformations of the Age Point passing into my first tenanted house, the 5th house and into the fiery sign of Leo."

First contact

As her Age Point entered the 5th house, Denise experienced her first direct contact with a planet. Up until then, all Age Point aspects had been more indirect, taking place as she travelled through the untenanted first quadrant. The exception had been the opposition to Saturn when she first visited Germany and met her beloved Omi for the first time, a connection and relationship which was strongly forged and which had a lasting positive effect on her life. The 5th house is the arena of relationships. It can be where we play the field, or test out the strength of our relationships and friendships with others, as well as where we might aim to impress them too. After moving through the empty first quadrant, Denise experienced the Age Point's transit of the 5th house very intensely because she met not just one, but three planets there, and in fairly rapid succession. She also made contact with Pluto, one of the pinning planets in the Animated figure, triggering the active potential of all the other planets involved in this aspect pattern.

She describes this period of life thus: "Perhaps part of the reason I experienced the Age Point in the 5th house so intensely was because of the contrast of its passage through 4 houses with no planets, and suddenly there were 3 of them – in a Fire sign (perhaps thankfully in a fixed house & sign!) – in aspect patterns (including the large quadrilateral), beginning and ending with a transpersonal planet. With this intensity plus Uranus, Venus and Pluto on the 5/11 Relationship Axis, it isn't surprising that relationship issues were intensified and were a focal point for transformation. This period was also one of travel, learning, new spiritual ideas, pain and loss. The foundation of my marriage was inadequate for us to grow together and to adapt to all the aforementioned changes. The bond between us just was not strong enough or deep enough to weather them all in addition to the physical time apart and the psychic distance created by our focus in totally different worlds – the academic and teaching one I was in and the commercial/sales work he was in. I think I could say my commitment to the marriage was faltering already by the time the Age Point reached Uranus, probably at the midpoint between the Uranus/Venus conjunction in the summer of 1981, when my mother and I travelled together to Germany. However there wasn't a dramatic shift away from my attention and affection for him, as the Uranus/Venus connection might suggest. I can now see that there was an invisible showdown, of sorts, between conditioning and convention, (which is what the marriage represented) and transformation. We tried counselling; it was hard for me to rationalize a split because, fundamentally, he was a decent and good person. In 1982-83, with my Age Point in the fixed zone of the house, I even considered switching universities and joining him in Chicago, but by this time I think I knew the relationship had no future and I was just going through the motions. Tradition and all that bound me to it was a powerful influence, together with prolonged indecision on my part. Perhaps this was also partly due to the influence of the Age Point moving through a fixed sign and house, and a reluctance to change. But, almost to the day of the midpoint between Venus/Pluto, the divorce was final."

Denise's Age Point journey through the 5th house continued. She was still teaching, specialising in German and Russian, and she focussed her attention on completing her doctoral thesis. She joined a meditation group, learned about Agni Yoga teaching, the creative art of Nicholas Roerich, and had her first encounter with the esoteric material and writings of Alice Bailey. In 1984, as her Age Point entered the 5th house Low Point, and suffering from burn-out, she moved and started a new job. At this time she also met F, who was to become her second husband. Of this experience she says: "I had briefly encountered the Alice Bailey material whilst working at the University, but it was F's connection with her books that really sparked my interest. It was his commitment to living by spiritual ideas, not just reading 'about' them, that really caught me and his enthusiasm for working creatively that inspired me."

In 1985, with her Age Point triggering the Animated figure by first making a square to Saturn, followed by a sextile to Neptune and finally coming to conjunction with Pluto, Denise became aware that there was something seriously wrong. Her health declined, this coinciding with her Age Point moving into the sign of Virgo. She was diagnosed with "incurable scleroderma", an autoimmune disease which affects the skin and connective tissues. She began a course of alternative treatments and by the time her Age Point had moved into the 6th house, she and F had decided to move south for the benefit of her health. Denise says: "Physically, I 'came to the end of my rope' just after the Age Point transited Pluto. I was already not well, but it was then that it reached a crisis point – the stress of the huge changes and activity and the shocks of the past few years took their toll. In this crisis, we did not resort to conventional treatment, which offered little to no hope of recovery, but turned to alternative medical treatment. It seems that the 5th house was full of small and large leaps of faith. Perhaps it isn't surprising to be affected so strongly, particularly physically, by this transit as it also activated the entire quadrilateral Animated figure from this point on – including a square to form-related Saturn. I did feel lucky to have survived, frankly."

Denise here summarises this active and eventful period of the Age Point moving into and through the 5th house of her chart in her own words: "The Age Point transit through the fixed 5th house had the effect of leaving almost nothing standing, in terms of what I brought into it from the 4th house. The assumptions of how things held together, from my first choice of partner, to plans for an academic future, a certain reliance on my family dissolving through the loss of my beloved Omi, to ideas about health, spirituality, financial security of any sort, conventional ideas of the future and past dreams. It was a sort of baptism by fire – so much burned away. It was impossible, with the transpersonal planets here, to hang onto much at all, but it meant entering Virgo and the 6th house wounded and worse for wear, but cleansed and looking for a bit of a respite, so that something new could emerge from the ashes."

* * * * *

Henri Cartier-Bresson: Image Maker

The next chart is that of iconic photographer Henri Cartier-Bresson. He was born in France in the early 20th century, just east of Paris in Chanteloup-en-Brie, close to where the EuroDisney resort is now located. He was the son of a wealthy textile family and was brought up in a formal French bourgeois atmosphere. He worked for the underground movement during the German occupation in World War 2. Having been taken prisoner of war he successfully escaped at his third attempt, going on to aid other escapees and work secretly with other photographers to cover the Occupation and then the Liberation of France.

Henri Cartier Bresson

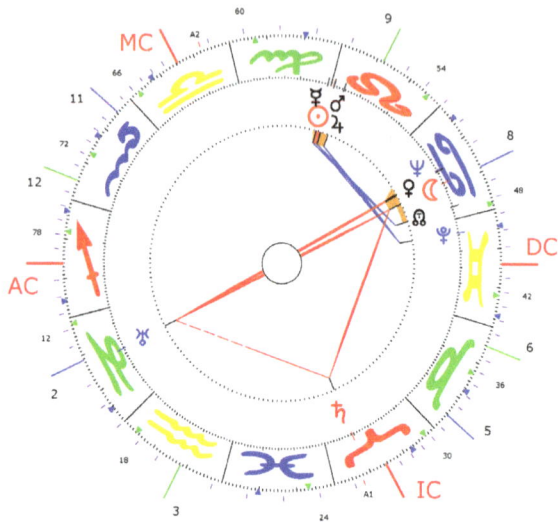

22.08.1908, 14:51, Chanteloup-en-Brie, France

Cartier-Bresson has a clear, uncluttered and almost sparse chart. Like an arrowhead diving down to the bottom of the chart, the only complete aspect pattern is an Achievement/Efficiency triangle. The key function of this figure is achievement through purposeful work. Composed of red aspects – two squares and the opposition – it has the capacity to work tirelessly. Saturn in Aries at the apex forms the focal outlet point for the cardinal energy inherent in this figure, highlighting the drive to manifest matter or form of some kind. The qualities of the pinning planets which hold the energy in tension along the opposition are interesting when viewed, as here, in the chart of an artist and photographer. Uranus opposes Moon, Venus and Neptune, all three of them "soft" planets which are associated with emotional, artistic and visionary expression. Nudged, prodded and activated by creative Uranus, strongly-placed on the 2nd cusp, all three planets would seek grounding and material expression via Saturn.

Age Point conjunct Uranus

Before he took up photography, Cartier-Bresson was a painter, and it was to this that he returned on his retirement. His interest in painting was sparked by an influential uncle when his Age Point approached conjunction with Uranus. He is quoted as saying "Painting has been my obsession from the time that my 'mythical father', my father's brother, led me into his studio during the Christmas holidays in 1913, when I was five years old. There I lived in the atmosphere of painting; I inhaled the canvases." Cartier-Bresson's early career followed an artistic path. He was a member of the Surrealist movement, and his work was influenced by these ideas. He studied painting under cubist André Lhote, which offered the theoretical training that helped him, in later years, resolve the challenges of marrying artistic form with photographic composition. Saturn at the apex of the Achievement/Efficiency triangle would undoubtedly have been involved here while the structure and organisation of the form he would eventually work with were perfected.

Cartier-Bresson's chart shows two distinct, separate and very different approaches to life. On the one hand, the triangular Achievement/Efficiency figure is a major focus of activity. Composed only of red aspects, and with a mutable motivation, it speaks of being adaptable, flexible and going with the flow of life, but with a goal in mind and a lot of underpinning energy, determination and drive to reach it (apex Saturn in Aries). The 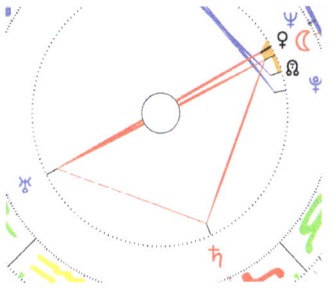 separate linear blue sextiles appear almost as an aside, a sub-plot to the main plot shown in the triangular Achievement/Efficiency figure.

Two modes of being

Linear aspects which do not form complete aspect patterns have a cardinal, sometimes erratic quality, yet these are all sextiles, not renowned for go-ahead energy because they are more passive and concerned with consolidation. The chart has no green aspects (semi-sextiles and quincunxes) to bring greater awareness to the activity-oriented triangular red figure, or the laid-back, more passive nature of the disconnected linear blue aspects. This suggests that Cartier-Bresson could have moved between two modes of being – active when working, creating and out in the field on photographic assignments, and passive when in more relaxed mode. In the 9th house stellium his Sun is in aspect to the Moon's Node, part of the 7th house stellium in his chart. It is the Node which links the two aspect configurations and the two separate modes of being.

Moon's Node and Age Point

Much of Cartier-Bresson's professional achievement as a photographer relates to significant Age Point aspects to the planets in the Achievement/Efficiency triangle, and to the Moon's Node in the 7th house. The North Node is a point of growth, situated in the house and area of life which often holds the greatest challenges for the individual. Bruno and Louise Huber say, "With every aspect to the Dragon's Head, there is a notable opportunity for further development". The challenges of a 7th house North Node will often be declined by the individual who has one in favour of the comfort of what is well-known and familiar in the 1st house. Here, it is independence which will be valued and not readily given up, and the person may be something of a loner, happy in their own company.

A 7th house North Node is described by the Hubers as one where it is important to "strike a balance between ourselves and others", an area of life where the person has to "dedicate himself to others so that further development can take place". Cartier-Bresson's professional work as a photographer depended on this approach; the subject matter he chose needed people. Although most of his photographs are of others (7th house) he retained a life-long aversion to being photographed himself, valuing his privacy (1st house).

In 1931, aged 21 and broken-hearted at the end of a love affair, he went to Ivory Coast, seeking adventure and escape. Here, he contracted blackwater fever and nearly died. Back in France, recuperating, he deepened his association with the Surrealists. His Age Point during this period was making a sextile to the Moon's Node, and this heralded a turning point for him. He saw a photograph taken by a Polish photojournalist of "black kids running in a wave", adding "I couldn't believe such a thing could be caught with the camera. I said damn it, I took my camera and went out into the street". He gave up painting and started to develop his photography, saying "I suddenly understood that a photograph could fix eternity in an instant." He acquired a Leica camera and travelled throughout Europe, photographing people living their everyday lives. He is quoted as saying, "I prowled the streets all day, feeling very strung-up and ready to pounce, ready to 'trap' life" – a telling comment from someone who had so recently almost lost his own life.

A Wealth of Age Point Aspects

Age Point aspects light up and activate the planets they contact and at the same time they animate the aspect patterns those planets are involved in. The years 1935 to 1939 were rich and fruitful as Cartier-

Bresson developed his career in photography. Amazingly, during this brief period his Age Point aspected every planet in the chart, beginning in 1935 when a sextile was made to the Moon/Venus/Neptune stellium at the time that he was invited to exhibit his work in New York.

Whilst the Age Point was busy squaring Jupiter, Mars, Moon and Mercury, trining Uranus, making semi-sextiles to Saturn and Pluto and changing signs from steady earthy Taurus to airy and communicative Gemini, Cartier-Bresson was busy learning the art of film-making alongside French film director Jean Renoir. He played a small part in one of the films, and Renoir is reputed to have insisted on this so that Cartier-Bresson would understand how it felt to be on the other side of the camera – a challenge to that 7th house North Node.

His first photojournalism pictures were published in 1937 when he covered the coronation of King George VI in London, taking no photos at all of the newly crowned king, but focussing instead on the crowds lining the streets who were hoping to catch a glimpse of him.

War years

The Hubers describe the fight for existence as a psychological stage of growth when the Age Point moves through the 6th house. This house is also the area of life where work and the justification for existence is played out. This period of Cartier-Bresson's life included enlisting for army service in World War 2, capture by the Germans and nearly 3 years spent as a prisoner-of-war, doing forced labour. His first two attempts to escape failed, but on the third try he made it, hid out while he obtained false papers, then joined the underground movement, helping other escaped POW's. In 1943, with his Age Point semi-sextile Moon and quincunx Uranus, the planet which had sparked his artistic interest and abilities, he dug up and once again began using his beloved Leica, which he had buried in farmland earlier in the war.

Sign Change

In 1947, Cartier-Bresson's Age Point moved from Gemini to Cancer. A change of sign is always significant when considering Age Progression. The Hubers say, "the basic outlook and motivation change according to the new sign qualities". The change from an air to a water sign brings less involvement and interest in airy, mentally-oriented matters and a greater awareness and consideration of feelings. Moving into the sign of Cancer, there is a stronger need to belong, to have a sense of group or family. Cartier-Bresson's chart has a strong emphasis of planets in Cancer, including the Moon, and as his Age Point moved into the sign he, along with three fellow photographers, formed

Magnum Photos, a cooperative picture agency owned by its members. The team shared assignments between them, each covering a specific area of the globe and aiming to use their photography in the service of humanity – a very apt and graphic example, in Cartier-Bresson's case, of his Age Point in Cancer.

Assigned to work in India and China with this cooperative, Cartier-Bresson gained international recognition for his coverage of Gandhi's funeral in 1948, and the final stage of the Chinese Civil War in 1948 – this as his Age Point was conjunct his North Node, picking up not only the stellium of planets in Cancer, but also the Achievement/Efficiency triangle which dominates his chart.

The Decisive Moment

In 1952, with his Age Point making semi-sextiles to both Jupiter and Pluto, Cartier-Bresson published his book *The Decisive Moment* (*Images à la sauvette*), a selection of his photographs taken in the East and West, with a cover designed and drawn by the artist Matisse. Of its title and his work, Cartier-Bresson is quoted as saying, "Photography is not like painting. There is a creative fraction of a second when you are taking a picture. Your eye must see a composition or an expression that life itself offers you, and you must know with intuition when to click the camera. That is the moment the photographer is creative", adding, "Oop! The Moment! Once you miss it, it is gone forever."

During the 1960s and early 1970s he continued to travel the world as a photojournalist, and had numerous exhibitions of his work. When his Age Point moved into the 12th house he began to move away from photography and concentrated on drawing. The Hubers say of the Age Point in the 12th that the person "gives up personal striving and the environment no longer challenges him. Only outstanding individuals are still capable of high achievements (political leaders, artists, scientists, etc.)"

Although retired as a photojournalist, he continued to work as an artist, returning to his first love, painting. He died in 2004, aged 95.

* * * * *

Kitty: Practicality in Action

I've known Kitty for some time as a trustworthy and reliable friend. She is both generous and practical. If help is needed she is always there to lend support, but being practical she is more likely to offer a home-cooked casserole than a bunch of flowers in times of need. Kitty is an excellent cook. Her career has covered working as a professional cook, as a local authority catering advisor in schools and colleges, and latterly as a lecturer in hotel management and catering. Her standards are high, and woe betide the manager of any hotel she stays in if there is something amiss, as she always reports it. As her friend, an invitation to a share a meal cooked by Kitty is a treat to be looked forward to.

I knew that Kitty was born with the Sun in Gemini, but I always had a strong impression of a lot of Taurus energy at work. She's an avid gardener who led a gardening group for several years, an accomplished seamstress and embroiderer, and she enjoys working creatively with food. A meal cooked by Kitty is always a pleasure to partake in. Therefore when I set up her chart I wasn't entirely surprised to see she has three planets in Taurus all close to the IC, rooting and grounding her firmly into the collective and forming a steady base in the chart from which she can reach out into the world.

Kitty

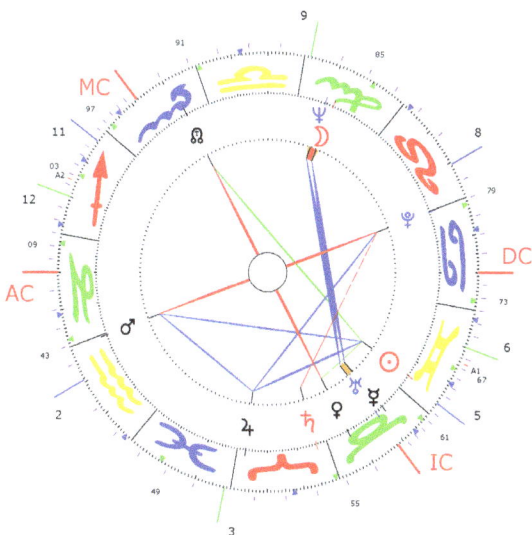

26.05.1939, 22:55, Sheffield, England

Kitty's chart does indeed have the appearance of her capacity to reach outwards and upwards, with aspects moving from the lower hemisphere like beams of light emerging from the almost complete asymmetrical container at the bottom of the chart. Kitty's overall chart shaping is mostly triangular with some disconnected linear trines, suggesting that her motivation is to adapt and go with the flow. Alongside this there is what could be a quiet restlessness, like a sub plot to the main event; her blue linear aspects are tangential and might want to do their own thing. But because the aspects are trines, and because they are connected by two conjunctions in the practical Earth signs of Taurus and Virgo, this restlessness may be more controlled and organised, and perhaps quieter. If Kitty feels she wants to branch out into something new and different, it's quite likely that she will research it well beforehand.

Aspect Patterns

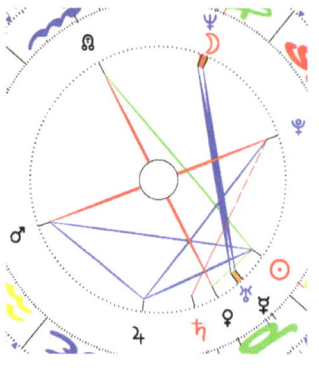

With a good balance of red, green and blue aspects, Kitty is able to conserve and direct her energy comfortably, focussing on the consolidation and enjoyment of what she achieves. The all-blue Small Talent triangle indicates the presence of a specific talent or skill which Kitty has been able to draw upon and use, perfecting this throughout her life. Pinned by Mars, Jupiter and her Gemini Sun, and with Jupiter at the apex in Aries in the 3rd house, it reflects her ability to teach, based on her own skills and extensive practical experience of working in hospitality.

Adjoining the Small Talent triangle is an Ambivalence triangle, with Jupiter once again a focus at the blue "escape" corner of this figure. Jupiter receives only blue aspects, emphasising Kitty's potential to be quite laid back about what she has gained and learned from her own experience and to use and share it with others in her professional life as a teacher. With an Ambivalence figure, the more restful motivation comes from the blue aspects and the planet at the blue corner – Jupiter in Kitty's chart. The other part of this figure – the red opposition – is where the person will be driven to act. In her chart the pinning planets in the opposition are Mars and Pluto, both on the 1/7 Encounter axis. You may be ahead of me here, and warning lights could already be flashing. If so, you'd be right; Kitty can be formidable when fired up, whether it's to get something done, or to stand up for a cause. With Pluto in the 7th house, albeit weak by sign and only just past the Low Point, she does not take prisoners.

Interestingly, Kitty has a separate red/green Irritation triangle cutting across her chart from top to bottom, which contains her Gemini Sun. From my own observations of Kitty, I've seen this aspect pattern swing into action alongside her formidable Mars/Pluto opposition. Generally speaking, an Irritation triangle can act like a whiplash, suddenly erupting and taking people by surprise when things get too much for the individual to bear. The person will have their say, get whatever was bothering them off their chest, and then return to a calmer state of mind. Kitty herself agrees that this is what she experiences when she "loses it". Her Irritation triangle behaves rather like a small green and red dagger which suddenly appears and then disappears. Normal service is resumed fairly quickly after the explosion and Kitty herself is back on an even keel.

Age Point in the First Quadrant

With Kitty's cooperation, I looked at the movement of the Age Point in her chart, and its first direct meeting with a planet. This took place as her Age Point moved through the first quadrant, always a significant time psychologically in the life of a young child as this is when the ego is established and the child learns to separate from the close protective care of the mother figure. I knew Kitty had a younger sister but wasn't sure when she'd been born. The Age Point conjunction with Mars seemed a likely time, since I was aware that Kitty and her sister had not always got on and that there had been some friction between them. Her sister was born when Kitty was four and half, on that conjunction with Mars – and along with it, the opposition to Pluto.

Kitty described how she'd had to be the older sister, and was expected to become more responsible. As her parents were busy running their own business, Kitty had to take on some of the care of her sister and she often felt resentment about this. She was only able to detach from this when older and she'd moved away from home.

At age 10/11, Kitty's Age Point was in Pisces and opposite the Moon/Neptune conjunction, connecting her with the linear trines which appear as the subplot in her chart. Here, another aspect of her personality was involved, with another mode of self-expression. At this time Kitty started dancing classes, learning tap, ballet and ballroom dancing – Pisces, Moon and Neptune being appropriate symbolically for the connection with self expression through dance. She loved this and became particularly good at ballroom dancing, as a teenager winning a wealth of cups in various competitions.

At the age of 13, with her Age Point in Aries and conjunct Jupiter, she learned to drive. By this time she had already been helping out in both the home and in the business her parents ran. They had a traditional grocer's shop in a small village. As their extended customer base was spread over several villages covering a wide area, they also had a mobile shop. Kitty helped her father with this aspect of the business after school and at weekends, and he taught her to drive the mobile shop van off-road. This Age Point conjunction coincides with Jupiter's placement at the apex of the Small Talent triangle; Kitty began to gain new experiences and added to her practical skills at an early age.

Her Age Point was conjunct Saturn when she reached the age of fifteen and half. Up until this time she'd been managing her school work alongside helping with the home and business after school hours. Saturn, placed at the bottom of the chart, can be an asset as it helps to ground the individual and makes them aware of their roots and provenance. Saturn can act as a teacher as well as psychologically giving us boundaries and making us aware of limitations. It also symbolises the sense of self we gain through the physical body. When her Age Point reached its conjunction with Saturn, Kitty was physically unable to sit her final school exams as she was suffering with severe hay fever. A doctor's letter had to be presented to the examination board to verify this, and she was allowed to sit the exams later in the school year.

Following this event, Kitty's Age Point first went through the 3rd house Low Point and then changed signs from fiery Aries – where life had been very busy – to earthy Taurus where she was to encounter the three planets in this sign between the ages of 16 and 20. At age 16, her Age Point was conjunct Venus. This connected her with the red/green Irritation triangle which also contains the Sun. At age 16, she also met Tom, who was to become her husband. Because this Age Point transit connected her with her Sun and with the Irritation triangle I asked Kitty if her relationship with Tom had helped her stand up for herself. She replied, "Yes – and to balance out activities like working in the family business, college studies and leisure."

Although there was great opposition from her parents, she and Tom stayed together and married soon after her Age Point had moved into Gemini. But before this, her Age Point crossed the IC at age 18, taking her into a new quadrant and into the very small 4th house. When the Age Point is in a small house, life can feel busy and hectic. Kitty had already felt the effect of her Age Point in Aries; there was no let up when it went into this small house, where with so much happening it can feel to the person as if their feet barely touch the ground. The Age

Point was also conjunct Uranus/Mercury, connecting her for the first time with the separate linear trine aspects in her chart. However, all was not well. Kitty's grandma, who she was very close to, died. Uranus can represent the grandmother, and in Kitty's chart the conjunction of Uranus with Mercury suggests an ease of communication between them. Her grandma taught her things and was there for her at times when her mother – involved in the business – was not.

The next two years were probably the most turbulent of Kitty's life. She married Tom in 1962, when she was 23. Their close friend, Roger, best man at their wedding, died suddenly the following year. The next year, 1964, Tom died after a short, debilitating illness. Kitty was 25. She'd been married for barely 18 months. During this period her Age Point had changed sign and house, and had approached and became fully conjunct her Sun, once again picking up the Irritation triangle as it had when she'd first met Tom. The Hubers say of conjunctions that, "Usually their ingress is marked by external events which can bring about marked changes in behaviour and lifestyle… positive changes activate inner powers…" and go on to say that "Aspects between the Age Point and the Sun present a challenge to autonomous thinking that could lead to self-development."

I asked Kitty if her outlook on life changed at this time, and if so, how? I wondered if she felt she was thrust into becoming more autonomous and what this felt like for her. Kitty responded by saying, "Life seemed very unfair at the time, but I had to plan a new life. I moved house, then job, in order to have more of a challenge. Meeting new people helped too, and gradually the hurt became less sharp."

Kitty's life moved on and in 1969, when she was 30, she married again as her Age Point moved into the 6th house and was making a square to her Moon/Neptune conjunction. She remains happily married, and I could say that this is where we leave her life story and Age Point journey, except that there may be some readers who are intrigued, as I was, at what her experience of Age Point conjunct Pluto had been. Pluto is in the 7th house, is opposite Mars and is part of the Ambivalence figure I've already referred to as demonstrating one manifestation of the Mars/Pluto in action. In 1979, when Kitty was 40, she'd taken time out of work to have her daughter, and with her Age Point conjunct Pluto and about to change signs and move from watery Cancer into fiery Leo, she trained to teach, changed jobs and moved on to become a lecturer in further education. An Age Point contact with Pluto does not necessarily have to be overly dramatic, but it can signify important inner changes. Pluto seeks perfection, and in order to reach this it demands we shed some of the old, outworn

102   Using Age Progression

attitudes and values we may be carrying as additional baggage. The Hubers say that at the time of an Age Point transit of Pluto, "…we become capable and willing to make change in ourselves… Pluto is always endeavouring to bring us to perfection as soon as possible".

* * * * *

Meryl Streep: A Class Act

The next example interpretation comes from the chart of actor Meryl Streep, who has won numerous awards, including three Oscars, during her long career which spans more than 40 years. I first heard her sing "God Bless America" in a quavery voice at the end of the film *The Deer Hunter* made in 1978; in 2008 she was belting out Abba songs in the hit film version of *Mamma Mia!* Research into her background reveals that her early performing ambitions leaned towards opera. Her ability to use her voice in song is something that has long been around, but she has focussed on stage and screen acting, and is widely regarded as being one of the most talented and respected movie actors of the modern era.

Meryl Streep

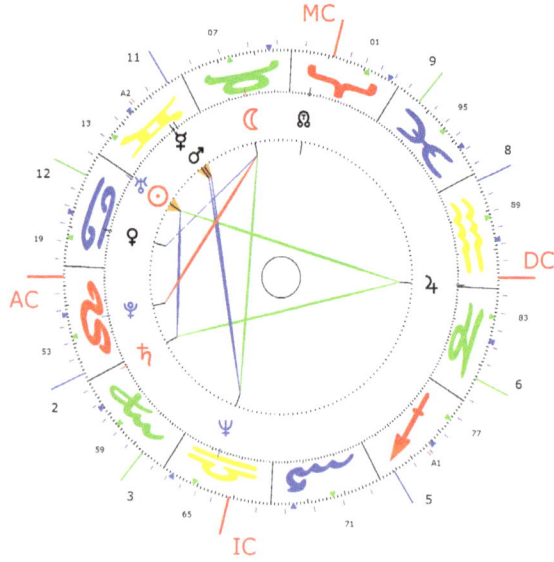

22.06.1949, 08:05, Summit, New Jersey, USA

Streep's chart image is reminiscent of the twitching nose of an inquisitive mouse emerging from a crack in a wall. Jupiter at the end of the nose seems to be probing pointedly and directly towards the DC and could be the first thing people pick up about Streep on meeting her. Jupiterian qualities of friendliness and benevolence, along with perception and an openness to new experiences are what she greets the world with. Jupiter would also be a valuable observational tool in helping her gain an understanding of how others live, which could then be ploughed back into her acting roles. It's also significant that Jupiter is at the apex of the Projection figure, but more of that later.

Streep's chart shaping and inner motivation is a combination of mutable and cardinal energy. This is indicated by the mixture of triangular aspect patterns and disconnected linear aspects present. She will be able to adapt and adjust to changing circumstances and go with the flow of life when operating in the mutable triangular figure which dominates the chart, yet she also has plenty of cardinal linear aspects which give go-ahead, goal-oriented motivation, and can be expressed as tangential or even erratic behaviour.

Streep has a colour balance of 1 red, 3 green and 3 blue aspects. Compared to the "benchmark" ratio of 3 red, 2 green, 6 blue, she lacks active cardinal red energy when set alongside her quotient of mutable green thinking/seeking energy and the fixed stability of blue, which will allow her to simply "be" and enjoy. Such inner motivation suggests that Streep may easily be drawn into escapist/imaginative mode (no bad thing for an actor seeking to assume a character or take on a role), but with her comparative lack of red she may run out of steam when she's busy. She will need time to recharge and stay aware of the dangers of burn out. Her 12th house Venus, in a one-way sextile to her intercepted Moon, may be an effective ally in helping her achieve balance and take some time out when this is needed.

The direction of Streep's aspect structure is a mixture of both vertical and horizontal. She will be able to make easy contact with others via the horizontal aspects, but there is a strong upward pull from the vertical aspects, most notably from the Moon, the highest planet in the chart. This may be problematic as it is intercepted; she may feel that the feedback she needs, together with her emotional needs, are not always recognised or understood. For an actor this could prove a significant challenge. Generally speaking an intercepted Moon, especially if it is the highest planet in the chart, requires a lot of feedback, praise and reassurance that its achievements have been recognised.

With most planets on the AC side of the chart Streep appears to be an essentially private person, willing to venture out and meet others using Jupiter, prominently positioned before the DC. Jupiter is the tension ruler of the chart and will act as the filter for all contacts and experiences that involve interaction.

Projection figure

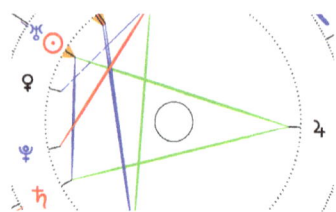

The Projection figure is the only complete aspect pattern in the chart, dominating the horizontal encounter axis. The aspect colours and motivation of this triangular, mutable figure are blue and green, with no cardinal red. The blue sextile provides substance; the green quincunxes bring searching and questing qualities, the ability to seek for answers and aim for long-term goals, underpinned with considerable awareness and sensitivity. The Projection figure is so-called, not because of an association with the psychological term "projection", but because the whole figure works like a slide- or film-projector. The planet at the apex is the projection source – here Jupiter – which transmits its qualities down the sensitive green quincunxes to the blue sextile aspect which forms the screen. The screen, in turn, receives and makes the imagined images visible, but always according to the planets which pin the ends of the screen. Here these are Saturn and the tight Sun/Uranus conjunction. Positioned as it is with the direction moving from Jupiter on the DC to Sun/Uranus and Saturn on the AC side of the chart, the Projection figure could lead to giving too much importance to the opinions of others.

I could easily argue that this aspect pattern, with its connotations of screen and projector, would make life a cinch for a film actor, but it's not as simple as that. In charts with this aspect pattern what has to be considered is whether projections are made consciously or unconsciously. Here I stick my neck out and assume that because of Streep's age, her breadth of experience and her success as an actor, she's using this Projection figure consciously, and as already mentioned, I think it would be of enormous value to her in the acting roles she undertakes. I vividly recall her performance in the film *Plenty* (1985) when she played the part of a cool English woman, changed forever by her wartime experiences as a Resistance fighter. Making her way in the post-war world she was without regard for who was hurt, or how. She spoke with a flawless cut glass accent and turned in a chilling performance. We can see the possible influence of meticulous Saturn at work here – concerned as ever with form and pinning one end of the screen of the Projection figure. But the Sun/Uranus conjunction at the other end of the screen brings invention, creativity and the ability to move outside the box and assume a wide variety of different roles.

The Hubers describe three different levels of the expression of the Projection figure. At the level of Emotional Perception, the conscious individual with this figure has "a wealth of ideas, imaginative vision and a remarkable talent for presenting things so that they can be communicated to others". And at the level of the Intellect, "people with this figure get both inspiration and a different awareness of many things in life". It is not difficult to appreciate Streep's talent and innate creativity working at both of these levels, tapping into the wealth of experience her prominent Jupiter contributes to her Saturn and Sun/Uranus in the Projection figure which dominates her chart.

Age Point Journey

Streep is an intensely private person, who refers to herself as "an actress who goes home to her family when I'm finished working", and there is little information available about her personal life. However, it is possible to speculate on her career in the context of Age Progression as there are some remarkable correlations between her career development and the movement of her Age Point. She made her professional stage debut in 1971 when her Age Point was in the intercepted sign of Scorpio in the 4th house, coinciding with its transit of Low Point 4. This is the life phase which tests and challenges the individual's ability to detach and move on from the safety of the family scene and make his or her own way independently in the world. The Hubers say "after the Low Point has been reached in the fourth house… the young adult ought to have learned to take charge of life, to trade punches with the world when necessary, and not to creep nervously under the parental roof for protection."

Picking up her Age Point in the 5th house in 1978 we can see how it relates to her career when she was 28/29. The Age Point had recently changed signs from Sagittarius to Capricorn. Moving from a fire to an earth sign – especially Capricorn – and edging towards the 6th cusp, this would have offered plenty of opportunities for ambitious hard work and knuckling down after its transit through Sagittarius. In 1978 her Age Point made an opposition to the Sun/Uranus conjunction and at the same time made a trine to Saturn and a semisextile to Jupiter. Whilst the trine and semisextile aspects have less impact in Age Progression, when viewed together, along with the opposition to Sun/Uranus, these light up the Projection figure and bring the potential of the whole pattern into play.

I see this figure as being instrumental in her success as an actress, with Jupiter on the DC acting as an invaluable observational and sensing tool which helps in her acting roles. In 1978 she was in *The Deer Hunter* which kicked off her career in films in an impressive way: she gained the National Society of Film Critics Award for Best Actress for her part in this and also received three other high profile nominations. When the Age Point is opposite a planet it can feel as if things are just slightly out of our control – the unforeseen can happen and we are swept along with the energy of the event. With the Age Point opposite both her Sun/sense of self and individuality, and creative Uranus, these events may have taken her pleasantly by surprise, but they would also have had the effect of strengthening her own determination to succeed. Her Age Point had just entered Capricorn and her Sun, with its tight conjunction to inventive, ground-breaking Uranus is involved. This, plus the first Saturn return as her Age Point made a trine to natal Saturn, brings hints of a double whammy at work here. 1978 was also the year she married the man she is still married to years later, and the year she was described as being "on the verge of national visibility".

The Sixth House

Streep was awarded her first Oscar in 1979 for *Kramer v. Kramer*, along with a whole raft of other awards and nominations too numerous to list. Her Age Point had just entered the 6th house, which coincides with the period of life when the person asserts and establishes themselves professionally in the workplace. Ages 30 – 36 in this house are a time of finding one's place and niche in life; in Streep's chart this is graphically emphasised with practical, hard-working Capricorn qualities forming the backdrop. Her Age Point in this period formed a quincunx to the Mars/Mercury conjunction in Gemini, placed in the cardinal zone of the 11th, between the cusp and Balance Point. Mars/Mercury in Gemini alone speaks of the potential for powerful communication. The quincunx from the Age Point carries seeking, thoughtful and perceptive energy, the effect being to strengthen the awareness and expression of the planets involved by bringing them more fully into consciousness.

In 1981, when her Age Point was on the Balance Point in the 6th house, Streep won acclaim for her role in *The French Lieutenant's Woman*. At the Balance Point of each house the individual on their life journey is able to smoothly and successfully undertake tasks associated with the house and the psychological life phase, expending what can feel like minimum effort for maximum rewards. The Balance Point is a place from which an accomplished and polished performance can be achieved – a juggler will not drop any balls, a cook will be creating new dishes without effort and an actress will be turning in faultless performances. 1982 saw Streep in *Sophie's Choice*, a harrowing tale of one woman's survival in a concentration camp, but at the cost of having to choose which of her two children is sent to the gas chamber. Streep is said to have done the choosing scene in one take as it was too emotionally challenging and draining to repeat. Her Age Point was opposite Venus in Cancer in the secluded 12th house of the chart. Venus also sextiles her Moon, pulling in a flood of emotional content. Here, Streep drew on her own personal feelings and emotions in order to channel them into her performance; as her first child was only 3 years old at the time this must have been an extremely poignant and difficult scene. She won numerous awards for her role as Sophie, including her second Oscar.

In 1985, Streep's Age Point travelled through the Low Point of the 6th house. This is a time, at age 34, when the person is forced to take stock of their career path and acknowledge what their limitations are and what they can and cannot realistically achieve. Although this can be a time of depression for some, those who approach this challenge with a degree of commonsense and personal awareness will come through it knowing that it is vitally important to make the right decisions for their career. In Streep's chart this phase benefits from the placement of optimistic Jupiter as the only planet in the 6th house, and the one awaiting the conjunction with the Age Point at age 35. This conjunction with Jupiter coincides not only with the Age Point's passage into Aquarius but it also lights up and activates the whole Projection figure and its pinning planets. The Age Point at the same time makes a quincunx to Sun/Uranus and Saturn which form the "screen" of this figure. Saturn's role suggests meticulous attention to the detail, with Sun/Uranus bringing invention and creativity to her work. It's interesting to see that at the same time, transiting Jupiter was conjunct her Saturn, and transiting Saturn conjunct her Sun, emphasising, along with her Age Point conjunct Jupiter, the significance of this aspect pattern in her chart as well as bringing complementary energies. These events coincided with her role as Karen Blixen in the epic film *Out of Africa*, for which she gained yet more awards.

Crossing the DC

The crossing of the Age Point over the DC at age 36 often heralds a new perspective on life. There's an awakening and realisation that there is so much more we can do, experience and achieve when the Age Point crosses the horizon and enters the conscious hemisphere of the chart. Opportunities abound here for self-realisation. Jung called the thirty-sixth year the "deciding year", a deciding point in life. Streep's career has been consistently successful on both sides of this point but it would be interesting to highlight a further few Age Point contacts of significance. In 1988, when she was 39, she was in *A Cry in the Dark*, taking the biographical role of Lindy Chamberlain, an Australian woman who was convicted of the murder of her baby daughter, although Chamberlain claimed that her daughter had been taken by a dingo. Streep's Age Point was appropriately opposite Pluto at the time.

In 2004, with her Age Point conjunct the unaspected 10th house North Node in ambitious Aries, she was awarded the Life Achievement Award by the American Film Institute. In 2006, aged 57, she once again picked up a long list of awards and nominations for *The Devil Wears Prada* with her Age Point conjunct the intercepted Moon in 10th. Acclaim for her role in the 2008 box office hit *Mamma Mia!* came as her Age Point moved out of intercepted Taurus and into Gemini, edging towards the 11th cusp as it made a trine to Jupiter, once again picking up the influence of the Projection figure which for me is a key consideration in Streep's chart.

* * * * *

David: The Warp and Weft of Life

David is a friend and fellow astrologer who has trained in the Huber Method. He has years of astrological experience under his belt and is also well-versed in esoteric astrology which he has studied for many years. David has tutored students of the Astrological Psychology Association as well as working as a counsellor and consultant astrologer with clients.

David's interests and skills are diverse, making him an interesting friend with whom I can not only discuss astrology, but plenty of other subjects as well. They cover a broad spectrum – astrologer, linguist, philatelist, accountant, musician, hill walker, fungi forager and esotericist. This diversity and activity is shown graphically in David's chart, which visually seems to hum with energy, and is reminiscent of vibrating strings.

David

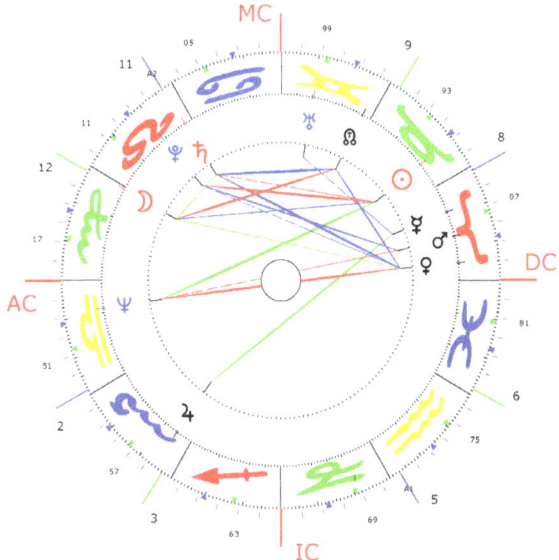

29.04.1947, 17:45, St. Andrews, Scotland

David's own image for his chart is of a weaving loom in action. A tapestry is being woven, the criss-crossing aspects being the warp threads with the separate linear aspect between Jupiter, Mercury and Uranus forming the shuttle which moves the weft threads back and forth, bringing the whole picture together.

There is an emphasis on the conscious, upper hemisphere, with only Neptune and Jupiter placed below the horizon. With a chart like this, he will have experienced most of the first 36 years of life, in the context of Age Progression, as a period when those things which happened to him were mainly out of his hands. He speaks of having no great sense of engagement at this time as he felt a lack of control accompanied by a sense of passivity. He felt that he was not in the driving seat of his life and as an only child, growing up in the 1950s, he was aware of having to live by the expectations of the time put upon him by his family.

David's chart shows a colour balance of 5 red, 4 green and 6 blue aspects suggesting that in the face of parental expectations, along with the feeling that he lacked control over what happened in his earlier years, he also has a high degree of sensitivity. Responses and reactions can come thick and fast from people with a high red/green aspect quotient. In David's case, Mars in Aries in the 7th house sitting alongside Mercury at the sharp end of the linear shuttle in the weaving loom image, would not need much encouragement to speak out. They would be fuelled, aided and abetted by this surfeit of red/green sensitivity and inner motivation. The linear shuttle, he says, acts independently. Disconnected from the main aspect structure – the warp – it can fly into action, sometimes making him outspoken to the point of bluntness when Mercury in Aries is engaged. At other times, Mercury can be fired up by creativity, new ideas and inspiration, drawing on its connections with Jupiter and Uranus.

The Recorder

Nestling in amongst the criss-crossing aspects – the threads of the tapestry – is a quadrangular aspect pattern, a Recorder, pinned by Venus, Moon's Node, Saturn and Moon. Made up of red, blue and green aspects, and positioned above the horizon, it has the potential to act in a fully conscious way. Its motivation is to seek security and stability because of its fixed shaping. There is an emphasis on blue aspects as it contains a Small Talent triangle. The other component patterns making up the Recorder are a Search figure and two Learning triangles. The Recorder therefore has great potential as it offers a large number of possibilities. People with this aspect pattern are able to record and store what is observed in the environment, picking up ideas and images from the situations they find themselves in, and ferreting out information which may be hidden or unnoticed.

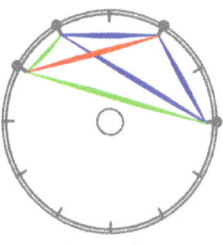

Recorder

Age Point Oppositions

The first logical step when looking at Age Progression in David's chart might be to consider the two conjunctions which would have occurred as the Age Point moved through the first quadrant of the chart – the conjunction of the Age Point first with Neptune and then with Jupiter. But this is a complex chart with the majority of planets above the horizon. We already know that he felt passive and under the influence of family expectations as a young child and teenager so it's more likely that the Age Point oppositions initially had a greater effect, but paved the way for the conjunctions which were to follow in later life.

David married at age 23 as his Age Point approached a change of sign and moved into the 5th house. The practical earthy sign of Capricorn was left behind and the freedom of Aquarius beckoned. These events coincided with David gaining his professional qualification as an accountant and with a complete new start for him in life. Not only did he marry, he also embarked upon a new career which took him and his wife to Africa. He describes this as his first experience of real independence; he was at last free from the expectations of his upbringing. In addition to the Age Point changing sign and house, an opposition to his cuspal 11th house Saturn was in place, together with a quincunx to his Moon. David has often spoken of his affinity with all that Saturn represents, and he has no fear of this planet and what it symbolises. At this opposition to Saturn he felt he was at last gaining control of his life, at the same time experiencing, via the quincunx to the Moon, contentment and personal happiness in his marriage.

Returning to his native Scotland a few years later, the Age Point first went over the 5th house Low Point, then was opposite Moon and stressed before the 6th house cusp. The 6th house brings career and the need to establish a foothold in this area of life into sharp focus, and at this stage David was struggling. With a young family to support there were financial difficulties. He made a career change and moved house as the Age Point entered the 6th house, squared the Moon's Node and was quincunx Saturn. His career was secured, but as the Age Point approached and crossed the DC he began to question what was important in life. Was it simply career success and a comfortable lifestyle, or was there more to life than this?

At age 37, with the Age Point in 7th house in Aries, and conjunct Venus, he began studying astrology. This sparked an interest in esotericism. David says that his Age Point crossing the DC was a very important time for him. As an adult he made the first conscious direct contact with a planet, Venus. This in turn triggered the potential of the Small Talent triangle in the Recorder as well as activating all the other pinning planets, bringing about a more conscious awareness of the 9th house Moon's Node at the apex of this figure.

Moon's North Node

The 9th house is associated with higher learning and when the Moon's North Node is there, the task for the individual is to move away from the South Node in the opposite 3rd house and to develop confidence in what we have already learned and what we know from our own experience. The 3rd and 9th houses are on the Thinking axis, and when the North Node is activated we can no longer rely on the ideas and opinions of the collective in the 3rd house. We have to stand up for what we know and have thought through for ourselves. For David, this was testing out and applying what he was learning in astrology alongside the more esoteric aspects of the subject. He describes this period when the Age Point was in Aries and making contact with first Venus, then Mars and Mercury, as a time of complete change in life direction. He became less materialistic as he was more financially secure, and his needs and interests changed correspondingly.

Neptune

Although this was an exciting and important period of life for David, all was not easy or well. His mother died the day before his Age Point conjunction with Venus was exact and this, together with the subsequent conjunction with Mars, brought him into contact with his 1st house Neptune. He has no recollection of any significant early life events when his Age Point was conjunct Neptune at age 2, but speaks of this planet having challenges for him in adulthood. Neptune on its highest level is about inclusive and compassionate love, not an easy state to achieve on a personal level at the best of times. With his mother's passing, David became responsible for the care and well-being of his father, who developed Parkinson's disease.

As his Age Point moved through the third quadrant, it directly activated all five planets there, including the Sun which is representative of the father figure in the Family Model as used in the Huber Method. David describes the quincunx between Sun and Neptune as uneasy and challenging, calling it a "green worm". The Sun is symbolic both of his father and of himself as an individual in his own right. David describes how his self confidence was undermined as he struggled to retain a sense of himself whilst caring for his father. Neptune at the other end of the "green worm" could produce feelings of his sense of self being dissolved. He says he had to hang on to his compassion in this situation, and he found it difficult to express his feelings to his father as his condition worsened and his care became more demanding.

Uranus, Saturn, Moon

The passage of the Age Point through the 9th house proved to be both rewarding and eventful for David. During this period it directly contacted first the Moon's Node and then Uranus. At this time David was involved in teaching astrology to groups in seminar and workshop settings, and he relished the challenges and satisfaction that live teaching brought. He was truly fulfilling the potential of his 9th house Node. At the Age Point conjunction with Uranus, David was made redundant and his career as an accountant ended. Rather than experiencing this as a blow David found it liberating. He used his deep understanding and knowledge of his own chart and of Age Progression to help him approach this new status with positive anticipation, likening it to the Chinese proverb "Crisis is danger and opportunity".

Things changed. David and his wife decided to downsize from the large family house where they had brought up three daughters, all now adults. They relocated to a scenic area in the Highlands of Scotland, and David describes the clearing of the house and subsequent move as incredibly easy. With his Age Point conjunct Saturn at this time, I'd thought it might be hard for him to let go and move on, but he speaks jokingly of what a relief it was to get rid of things which had accumulated over the years. This might sound more like the Age Point conjunct Pluto, but it was not. David's Saturn is strongly placed on the 11th cusp, and in his moon node chart is also in the same position; meeting with Saturn in this way in both charts he was on familiar territory. There was nothing to fear as he knew he was doing the right thing. With his admitted affinity with Saturn and to liking things being well-organised, this was a time of assurance that he was in control and answerable to no-one but himself.

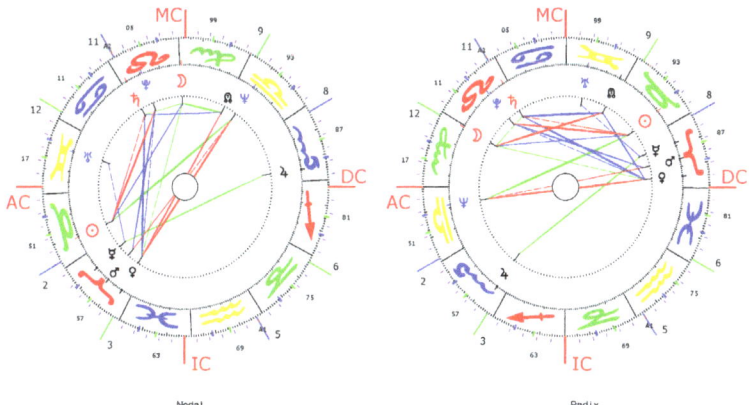

David's Moon Node and Natal Charts

David's most recent Age Point conjunction has been with his Moon on the 12th cusp. This coincides with feelings of joy for him as he has become a grandparent for the first time. His three daughters are all settled emotionally with their respective partners, and David is enjoying a sense of release from his concerns about them. This, in turn, is releasing for him the energy of Moon, and Neptune too, to enjoy his grandson and become the kind of grandfather he wants to be – just for himself.

* * * * *

Suzanne Fischer: A Passion for Music

Suzanne is a young woman with a blossoming a career as in international opera singer. I've known her for some time as she is the granddaughter of friends who live nearby. As a teenager she immersed herself in stage work and dance. She studied music from an early age, performed in youth orchestras and choirs and is an accomplished pianist and cellist. I first saw Suzy perform in a local high school production of *Les Miserables* where her stage presence stood out. Even then I was asking for her autograph before she became famous. I now have the autograph on a CD recording she's made, along with her birth data and her permission to use her chart in this book.

Suzy comes from a musical family. Her grandparents are retired professional musicians. Her great-grandmother played the violin, both her parents are professional musicians and her uncle is a composer and recording artist. Music is undoubtedly in her genes and has always had a strong presence in her life. Suzy says, "I am passionate about music. Some of my first memories and most profound moments include long hours listening to the sounds of music streaming out from my family's lives."

Suzanne Fischer

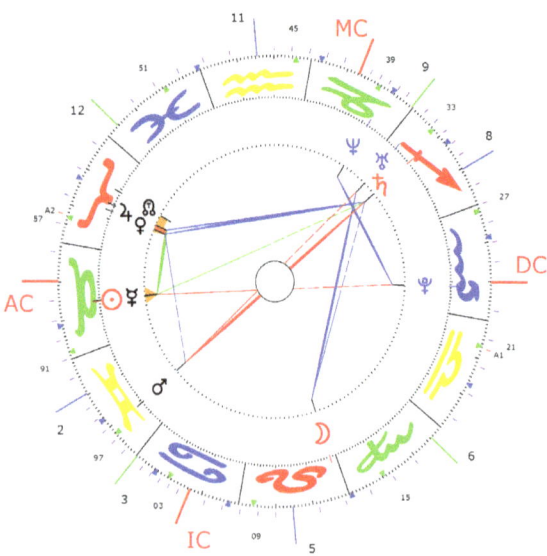

07.05.1987, 05.15, London, England

The visual image in Suzy's chart reminds me of a performer of some kind, maybe a juggler or tightrope walker, and there is a sense of movement and of balance being maintained. The chart shaping and motivation combines mutable triangular figures with some disconnected linear aspects, making her flexible and adaptable but with a restless, forward-looking enthusiasm for new challenges. The overall aspect structure is predominantly horizontal, suggesting she is oriented towards contact with others. Suzy is friendly and outgoing but she agrees she has a strong need for time alone too. This awareness is relatively newfound, and she is learning to relish the time she spends alone. Here I am looking at her "I" sided planets, and her Taurean Sun in the 1st house. Taurus is associated with singers and is the sign which rules the throat, and Suzy's Sun – her sense of self – is closely conjunct Mercury, with its drive to communicate. Following the horizontal direction of the chart my eyes are drawn to the Sun/Mercury conjunction opposite Pluto on the DC. To me this suggests, on one level, "Don't mess with this lady". She has a lot of powerful potential, both in her voice and personally, and she may well speak her mind, pulling no punches. She will not suffer fools gladly in her personal life, yet when she needs to, in her profession as a singer, she can draw on the energies of Pluto to embody and channel strong and powerful emotions, using her voice as the instrument.

Venus and Jupiter

The 12th house planets and the Moon's Node, all in Aries, are intercepted. Intercepted planets – those in a sign with no house cusps – need a conduit to the outside world as they are less able to express themselves successfully, and this could be doubly frustrating for Aries planets. A conjunction of Venus and Jupiter can suggest the capacity to expansively embrace, experience and express beauty and harmony. Of course, that is only one way of interpreting this 12th house conjunction. How it is experienced and expressed by the individual concerned will be shaped by environmental influences as well as by innate talent. Suzy says of music that she wants to "make this art form an integral part of my life", but in another chart, for another person and another life experience, Venus/Jupiter in the 12th house could, for example, indicate over-indulgence in the good life to the point of satiety.

Suzy's Venus/Jupiter conjunction forms a focal point for both aspect patterns in her chart – a Search figure and an Ambivalence figure. The presence of the Moon's Node in this conjunction highlights the importance

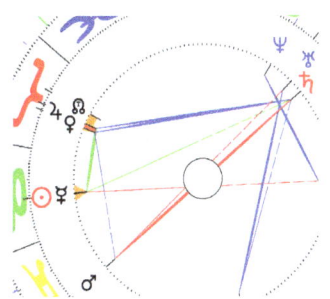

of Suzy developing this area of life for her own benefit and personal growth. She already has a busy schedule of training and performing, so it could be easier for her to focus more on the other end of the nodal axis – the 6th house where she'd be working and in contact with others – and neglect taking time out for herself to hone her musical skills as well as recharge her batteries. Suzy says, in response to this, "Correct! I am useless at putting time aside to be still and calm and look after myself. I have to force myself to do other things which give me calm time that isn't focused on music." In the Search figure Venus and Jupiter are at the blue/green corner of this pattern, whose motivation is to be on a lifelong quest to find perfection. Often the planets at this corner of the figure provide the outlet for what is being sought. But Suzy's Venus and Jupiter are intercepted, and need the other planets they aspect to help them in this task. Here she can draw on Sun/Mercury, Mars and Saturn to help her express the energies and qualities of Venus/Jupiter.

These planets also form the blue corner of the red/blue Ambivalence figure, which has an on/off approach to work and relaxation. When in the blue part of the figure – in Suzy's case, when she's immersed in her music, standing her own sense of self aside, as she says she needs to in order to allow the music to sing through her – she is doing something she truly loves and enjoys. Singing may not feel like work to her as it offers her a connection with her soul and her innermost self. She responds, "You're right, music certainly doesn't feel like work! That's why it's hard to stop and do other things." When she's in the red part of the figure – the Mars/Saturn opposition – the businesslike, working area of the figure springs into action. Spanning the fixed 2/8 axis, and pinned by Mars and Saturn, this part of the figure reflects the strong dedication and determination that Suzy has to reach her goals, as well as the practicalities of making a living for herself in her chosen career.

Significant Planets

As might be expected there was no specific memory for Suzy of her Age Point conjunct Mercury/Sun when she was still a baby, but she recalls that at age 2 she was taken by her father to her first music lesson, which was musical play. Here she has vivid memories of a colourful toy horn, and this first introduction to hands-on experience of music coincides with her Age Point being semi-sextile Mars and quincunx Saturn, bringing her into first contact with these two significant planets.

When Suzy was 8 years old, her Age Point was conjunct Mars, and this brought her in direct contact for the first time with the Ambivalence figure, connecting her life experience at that time to pinning planets

Saturn and the Venus/Jupiter conjunction. She recalls of this time, "I had an obsession with the melody of Jupiter from Holst's *Planets Suite*. I used to demand being taken by my Mum to Thursday night concerts at the Hallé concert hall, but this wasn't always allowed as I was too young." As her Age Point entered the mutable zone of the 2nd house and moved towards the 3rd house cusp, Suzy started learning to play the cello and piano. Her Age Point was quincunx transpersonal planets Neptune and Pluto as music flooded into her life and she says, "I remember sitting outside my Dad's bedroom just listening to him practice whilst he played the cello. I loved lying under Grandma and Poppa's bed in London listening to Poppa practicing the clarinet. Other moments are mainly of the Barbican concert hall, one in particular watching Dad and Poppa on stage playing at a London Symphony Orchestra kids' concert, with distinct memories of flying teddy bears and singing about a teddy bear's picnic…!"

When Suzy was 10, her Age Point was opposite Uranus and this brought an unexpected and traumatic bolt from the blue into her life. Her father emigrated to Australia and this year was one of major changes. With her Age Point in the 1st quadrant, Suzy had to learn how to adapt and survive in her changing world, and she began making some big decisions. She and her brother travelled to Australia to visit their father in the summer holidays after Suzy had left her primary school and was preparing to go to secondary school. She says, "In the final leavers' assembly of primary school I got up on stage, taking my turn amongst the other pupils, saying 'I am going to be a musician', holding up a violin case." She had publicly stated her intention .

At 11 she began singing and playing in youth choirs and orchestras. Her Age Point, still just in the 2nd house, was making a sextile to her Moon in Leo, the planet it is approaching now as her career changes gear and she moves into the fast lane. Music was becoming an integral and emotional part of her life. Of the time when her Age Point was opposite Neptune she says, "I remember being moved to near tears in youth orchestra, probably around the age of 16. Can't for the life of me remember what it was now, perhaps Rachmaninoff symphony number 2, and also Schubert, the 'unfinished' symphony."

At age 17, with her Age Point sextile her Taurean Sun/Mercury conjunction, and square Venus/Jupiter, Suzy was accepted to study at a prestigious ballet conservatoire in London. But the opportunities this promised were not to be. Suzy became ill and was unable to take up this place, but as her Age Point crossed the IC and moved into the 2nd quadrant, her life and musical aspirations took another direction. Instead of going to London she studied music and singing at Edinburgh University. At age 19, she started singing *lieder* (romantic solo songs) and opera as her Age Point, now in the 4th house, was once again semi-sextile Mars and quincunx Saturn. This time she'd picked up the hard-working opposition in the Ambivalence figure pinned by these two no-nonsense planets, but with some life experience behind her and an ever-clarifying goal before her. In her own words, this was a time when "all the different disciplines I had studied came together. Suddenly everything made sense and I knew what I had to do." She had found her vocation and her voice and she wanted to sing.

Saturn

To date, Suzy's CV of musical training, experience, performances and opera roles is long and impressive. I've seen her in live performance and can hear how her voice continues to develop. She has come a long way since I saw her in *Les Miserables*, and there is yet more to come. Like David in the previous chart example, Suzy does not shy away from Saturnian matters. She is able to use this planet at a conscious level as she is organised, reliable, dedicated and realistic, with a structured approach to reaching her goals. Her Saturn is comfortably placed in the fixed zone of the 8th house and along with Mars in the Ambivalence figure, it plays a significant role in her life and her developing career. She is unlikely to over-reach herself and is very aware of the importance of using control – an attribute of Saturn – in a positive way. Suzy says, "I know it's OK to go against the grain. I have persistently pushed my boundaries, learning new languages and cultures." Her dedication to her goal of becoming an opera singer has taken her to Milan, where she studied singing and learned Italian, and to Berlin to learn German. Fluency in both languages opens up the potential for more opera roles and for being employed in these countries without language difficulties.

Saturn, at its highest level, is often like a mentor or wise older person who acts as a guide and inspiration to the seeker. Suzy found her personal mentor when she was 25 and her Age Point was trine Saturn. She sought out a world-famous opera singer, auditioned for her and went to stay with her in Turin for intensive lessons. Suzy says, "Being taught by L.C. was life changing, I think, because she taught me to take control. I learned I couldn't let 'things' technical or otherwise, happen to me, and that I could make a decision and determine how I wanted to sing, what I wanted to express. And that anything less than that was not enough." She describes this as a life-changing experience which transformed her into the beginnings of the artist she now feels she is growing in to.

Suzy's Age Point entered the sign of Leo when she was 21 and is fast approaching conjunction with her Moon. This sign is often associated with the performing arts, her Leo Moon a strong indicator of her enjoyment in sharing her love of music. The conjunction with her Moon coincides exactly with her beginning her studies at a leading European music conservatoire in Berlin, taking up a place which was specially created for her. She is already preparing for four major opera roles; with her current Age Point conjunct her Moon and trine Saturn, Suzy is realistically grounded but is also very excited about this new phase of her career. She sums this up in her own words, "I have dedicated myself not only to good singing, but to being a complete artist who understands ballet, contemporary dance, stage craft, straight theatre and musicology. I do not believe it is enough to do anything less."

* * * * *

Alan Turing: Father of Computer Science

Bletchley Park in Buckinghamshire, UK, is the historic site of the secret British code-breaking activities which took place during World War 2. It is also the birthplace of the modern computer. For many years, Bletchley Park was not accessible to the public, but the entire site and its buildings is now a national museum which tells the story of the famous Enigma machine along with tales of spies and the work which was undertaken there during the war years. On my first visit I was fascinated by the exhibition on the life of Alan Turing, who was instrumental in creating and developing the modern computer. As his accurate birth data was available, I set up his chart.

In 1999, Time Magazine hailed Alan Turing as one of the hundred most important people of the 20th century for the part he played in creating the modern computer and making it a part of everyday life throughout the world. They said, "…everyone who taps at a keyboard, opens a spreadsheet or a word-processing program is working on an incarnation of a Turing machine".

Turing is widely acknowledged to be the father of computer science. During the Second World War he was a major contributor in the top secret work carried out at Bletchley Park. Here, he was involved in breaking ciphers, developing the Bombe – a cryptanalytic machine – which was able to decode complex messages sent by the German Enigma machine. It is said that his contribution, together with the work of countless others working at Bletchley Park, saved many lives and shortened the length of the war by 2 years.

Alan Turing

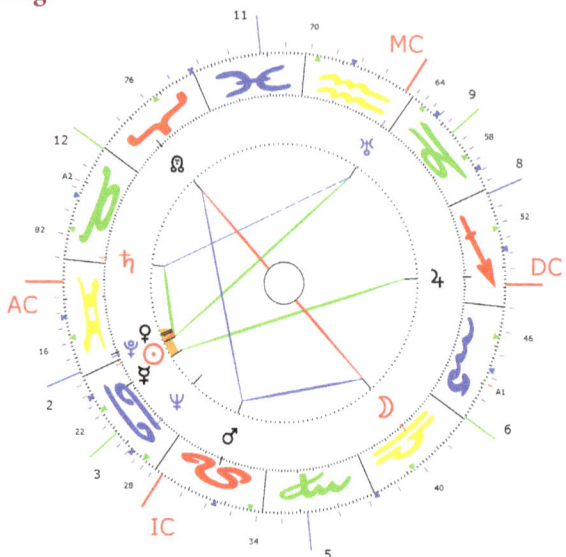

23.06.1912, 02:15, London, England

Alan Mathison Turing was born in London. His father was a member of the Indian Civil Service, and his ex-pat parents returned to England for his birth.

The Metronome

Turing's chart has a clear, angular appearance with two separate aspect patterns moving in different directions. Visually, his chart has a precise, mechanical appearance, reminiscent of a metronome ticking in strict time. The overall chart image can sometimes convey the essence of the person, and in this case it does; Turing's life was dedicated to the precision of mathematics, cryptanalysis and computer science.

His chart shows a lack of activity-oriented red aspects with only one – the opposition, where energy is held in tension – but this lack is compensated for by the stellium of planets on 2nd cusp, acting as a powerful generator and springboard for his intellectual genius.

Turing's chart has an emphasised "I" side, with a total of 7 planets in the AC hemisphere. A person with such a configuration would tend to be something of a loner, or be very selective about who they allowed into their life as a trusted friend. Yet Turing has Jupiter in Sagittarius close to the DC and in 7th house, which could be interpreted as indicative of optimistic, outgoing sociable behaviour. But look again. Turing's Jupiter is in a linear quincunx relationship with Mercury, itself part of that powerful stellium. Whilst Mercury endows a speedy fact-finding ability, when working in tandem with Jupiter there is an endless testing out of ideas and a gathering of experiences against which such ideas sink or swim. Linked as Mercury and Jupiter are by a quincunx, itself indicative of a big step in learning, it is more likely that his Jupiter in 7th would have been engaged in the discussion and testing out of ideas with others of like mind, rather than as a vehicle for outgoing sociability.

Nodal axis
A quick check on the position of his North Node in 11th opposite the South Node in 5th conjunct Moon would support this hypothesis. The South Node is not shown in Huber-style charts as it points to the past, to no growth and stagnation (Dragon's Tail) as opposed to the North Node which leads the way forward (Dragon's Head). Rather than moving from South to North Node to gain a balance between both ends of the nodal axis, some people live exclusively in the North Node. An 11th house North Node speaks of intellectual, like-minded and carefully selected friends who share ideas, ideals and interests which are far removed from the more earthy, tactile, rough and tumble of 5th house relationships. The Hubers say of the 11th house, "…it is a fundamental frame of reference… for doctrines and creeds;… for in 11th house conditions rather than processes hold sway." It is likely that Turing, with his keen intellect and mathematical mind, would have sought contacts of a similar sharp mindset in 11th rather than risk boredom and the challenge of physical contact in the more mundane 5th.

Yet matters of the 5th house, where his intercepted Moon is conjunct the South Node, did play a critical part in his life as he was homosexual at a time when this was illegal in Britain. He was briefly engaged to a Bletchley Park co-worker and fellow mathematician in 1941, when his Age Point was conjunct his Moon and South Node. Although he confessed his homosexuality to his fiancée, who was reportedly unconcerned, Turing decided that he couldn't go through with the marriage and the engagement was terminated. It would seem that he had, in his brief engagement to a fellow (11th house) mathematician, been seeking to connect with 5th house matters and energies and bring about a balance on the 5/11 axis of relationships

Turning to the aspect patterns which dominate his uncluttered and metronome-like chart, we can see that there are just two: a Search Figure and an Ambivalence figure. Both are interesting their own way, but it is the Search Figure which expresses much of the main plot of Turing's life.

Search Figure

Search figures are triangular, with mutable motivation. The direction and scope of the search is fluid, the person being able to change direction and follow the leads that arise during the search process. There is no fixity or rigidity involved; the individual is motivated to seek and search and will go where the journey takes them.

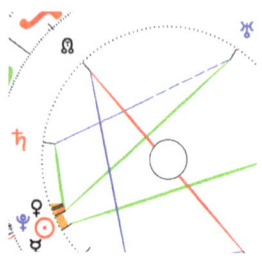

Composed of blue and green aspects, the Search figure – and the person who has one – is bound up in thoughts, ideas and an ongoing search which often has an "if only…" quality about it, as in "If only I can find the answers to [such and such] I will be happy and satisfied". Of course, the searching doesn't end and the quest itself is the spur and the drive. The Hubers say that people with this figure are "suited to working on long-term projects and can wait patiently until success comes of its own accord. They work continuously with the same dedication as at the start and know that everything takes time."

Experience suggests that the planet at the blue/green corner of this figure is the one which offers a possible outlet and expression for what is learned during the search. In Turing's chart, the planets pinning the corners of the Search figure are his Sun (part of the powerful stellium), Saturn and Uranus. Here we have a stunning combination of creative mental energies in Sun and Uranus, together with the potential for grounding and manifesting these via Saturn at the blue/green corner. What is more, practical Saturn is placed, albeit weakly by sign, in equally practical Taurus, and Uranus is comfortably on home ground in Aquarius.

World Improver

Bruno Huber called Uranus "The World Improver", the planet which represents creative intelligence, generating original ideas and looking for "systematic ways of solving life's problems". Uranus is the highest planet in Turing's chart, and is very strongly placed on the MC. It came as no surprise to see its position in Turing's chart, given his contribution to the development of the Bombe code-breaking machine and his role in the creation of the modern computer. Bruno Huber continues, "Uranus seeks knowledge for its own sake. It is the spirit of investigation that looks for suitable solutions to existing problems. Brainwaves happen [on the mental level]. Uranus breaks into the consciousness in the form of ideas that did not exist before, but that can change the entire situation at one stroke… the creative intelligence can usually break through in times of need… that is why Uranus finds its greatest satisfaction in righting wrongs and improving conditions." This suggests that strategic problem solving of all kinds was life blood to Turing, from 11th house games of chess with friends and colleagues, to 12th house back room activities when he was head of Hut 8 at Bletchley Park, devising techniques for breaking German ciphers during World War 2. International Chess Master Hugh Alexander, who worked alongside Turing at Bletchley Park wrote, "… if anyone was indispensable to Hut 8 it was Turing. The pioneer's work always tends to be forgotten when experience and routine later make everything seem easy…"

The inclusion of Turing's Sun in this Search figure is also significant. The Sun is representative of the individual's sense of self gained through the mind, the use of the will, the creative mental processes and the decisions made. Empowered in the stellium by Pluto, softened by Venus and egged on by Mercury, his Sun brings their additional input to the searching, questing and problem solving which drives this figure. All four planets in this stellium are either cuspal or strongly placed in 2nd; his most important possession was his mind.

Turing's Life Clock shows his Age Point conjunct this stellium at age 6, when he started school. His headmistress spotted his talent and signs of genius early on, as did many subsequent teachers.

Ambivalence Figure

The Ambivalence figure is perhaps more of a sub plot in his chart and what is known of his life. Although relationships are highlighted in his chart through the nodal axis, his Moon – his emotional sense of self – is intercepted in 5th house which suggests difficulties in expression and recognition of emotional needs. Indeed, as homosexuality was illegal at that time to come out about this would have attracted disapproval at the very least.

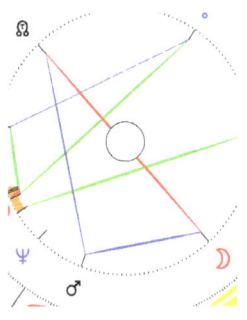

The red/blue Ambivalence figure is also triangular, having a mutable mode of action and the ability to swap between contrasting modes of activity when in the red aspect, and passivity when in the blue aspects. These blue aspects provide the opportunity to relax, with the planet at the apex acting as an escape point where the person can use and express its qualities. In Turing's chart this planet is Mars in Leo, positioned on the Balance Point of the 4th. A Balance Point planet can be expressed easily and with apparently little effort. There is not much information about Turing's off duty activities, but I was fascinated to read that he was physically very active, sometimes to the point of fanaticism. He was a keen cyclist, and while working at Bletchley Park, was a talented long-distance runner, sometimes running the 40 miles to London when called there for high level meetings. He is also reputed to have been capable of world-class marathon running.

Post-war years
Although Turing was awarded the OBE in 1945 for his wartime work and service, his work and what went on at Bletchley Park was kept secret for many more years. Churchill called the Bletchley Park staff "The goose that laid the golden eggs but never cackled". But since the opening of Bletchley Park to the public in 1993, the work of Turing and the other 8,500 people who worked there in total secrecy has become widely known.

In the post-war years, whilst his Age Point was opposite Saturn, Turing worked on the design of the Automatic Computing Engine. Again using his 12th house Saturn, he helped to bring into being yet another brainchild of the Search figure. In 1949, with Age Point conjunct Jupiter, he became Deputy Director of the computing laboratory at the University of Manchester, where he worked on software for one of the earliest stored-program computers, the Manchester Mark 1, and also on artificial intelligence. During this period, as his Age Point moved through Sagittarius, he developed an experiment known as the Turing Test, which sought to define a standard by which a machine might be called "intelligent". He also started to devise, with a colleague, a chess program for a computer.

In 1952, with his Age Point on the Low Point of 7th house, Turing began working on mathematical biology, specifically on morphogenesis – the study of the biological process which cause an organism to develop its shape. The Low Point is often a time of inner reflection; in the 7th Low Point is a time when the current lifestyle is revised and we question whether we have, to date, lived our lives fully. It can also be a time of partnership crisis.

An encounter in Manchester at this time between Turing and a man called Arnold Murray, and their subsequent relationship, led to a major crisis in Turing's life as both men were charged with and convicted of gross indecency. Given the choice between going to prison or being on probation and undergoing hormonal treatment to reduce his libido, Turing chose the latter. He was chemically castrated by oestrogen hormone injections, his security clearance was removed and he was barred from continuing his cryptography consultancy with GCHQ, the Government Communications Headquarters, a British intelligence agency.

With his Age Point moving through the mutable zone of the 7th house, from Low Point to the 8th cusp, Turing continued his work on morphogenesis. When his Age Point was exactly opposite Pluto, in the 28th degree of Sagittarius and within seconds of the 8th cusp, he committed suicide by cyanide poisoning on 7th June 1954. A partly-eaten apple was found beside him, and although it was never tested for cyanide, it is thought that this was the means by which he delivered himself of this fatal dose.

In Dane Rudhyar's book *An Astrological Mandala*, his keynote words for the 28th degree of Sagittarius offer an interestingly appropriate epitaph which nods very strongly towards Turing's Uranus on the MC: "The enduring elements in a society which reveal its ability to *significantly link the genius of its individuals to the everyday needs of the collectivity*". (my italics)

In 2009, following a successful petition campaign urging the British government to posthumously apologise to Turing for prosecuting him as a homosexual, Prime Minister Gordon Brown released an apology, "…on behalf of all those who live freely thanks to Alan's work I am very proud to say: we're sorry, you deserved so much better". Yes, he did.

The full, signed apology is on display at Bletchley Park, in the section devoted to honouring the genius of Alan Turing.

* * * * *

Imogen: A Healing Touch

Imogen is a friend. She can be deceptively quiet, but once you get to know her a person of depth, integrity and humour emerges. In her leisure time she enjoys walking and outdoor pursuits but in recent years has been concentrating on training to become a teacher of the Alexander Technique, a discipline for improving mental and physical function. This training has been intensive and over the past 4 years Imogen has been working in a full time job alongside the training. Her chosen aim – to become a fully qualified Alexander teacher – has been reached and she qualified with honours. She has set up her own part-time practice and has been invited to study to become a trainer. She is currently taking a professional development course to enable her to train others to become teachers of the Alexander Technique, and in the next year hopes to take on apprentice learners and to act as their tutor. Imogen describes her discovery and subsequent training in the Alexander Technique as being of immense importance in her life.

Imogen

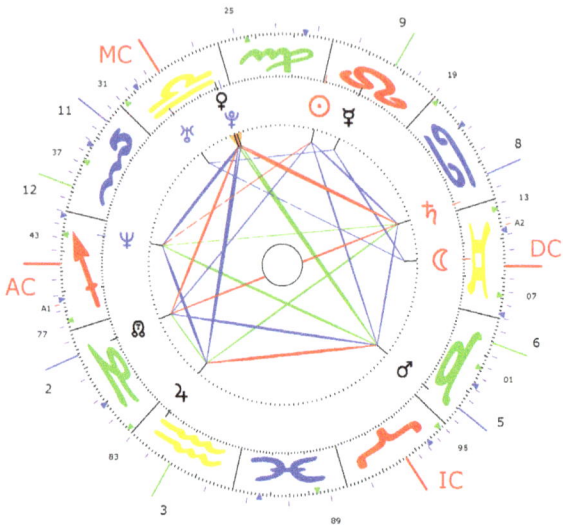

22.08.1973, 16:08, Manchester, England

Imogen's chart is complex and Imogen agrees she is a complex person. The chart contains one of the rarest aspect figures, a Pandora's Box. This five sided pentagon is composed of many identifiable aspect figures which combine in this large fixed structure to form a multi-faceted pattern with four searching green quincunx aspects at its core.

Pandora's Box and Small Talent Triangle

When first looking at Imogen's chart, many other identifiable aspect patterns begin to emerge, but these are largely component parts of the large, complete Pandora's Box. The Pandora's Box lies across the horizontal axis of her chart, with Neptune at the top of the blue lid on the 12th house Low Point. A Pandora's Box is encased in red/blue aspects, so when viewed from the outside it gives the impression of life lived in a clear cut, either/or way. Inside are the long green quincunxes, filling the box with questions, doubts, diverse interests, a depth of feeling and an interest in a variety of subjects. From outside, the person with a Pandora's Box

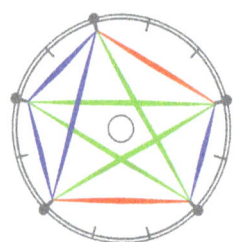

Pandora's Box

can appear calm, laid back and even inscrutable if the box remains closed; if it is opened up a rich and deep inner world becomes visible, surprising those who only see what is shown on the surface. The pinning planets on the corners of the box indicate how the Pandora's Box might operate, and what might be found inside. Imogen is interested in imaginative and creative pursuits which include healing, mysticism, music and science, and she has a long term love of history. An initial assessment of pinning planets Jupiter, Mars, Saturn, Venus/Pluto and Neptune can all be related to these pursuits.

Sitting completely separately is a blue Small Talent triangle spanning the 3rd quadrant of the chart. This is not connected to the main large aspect structure, and literally sits outside the box – the Pandora's Box that is. Pinned by Moon, Mercury 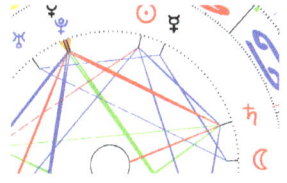 and Uranus, this aspect figure embodies behaviour patterns which differ from those in the Pandora's Box, but are complementary to it. The Small Talent triangle indicates a latent, seedling talent which can be developed, but it is also something which has to be worked at, encouraged, practised and nurtured so it can reach its full potential. Imogen's Age Point has most recently crossed the DC and been conjunct the Moon, the first of this figure's pinning planets that it has made direct contact with.

I first looked at Imogen's chart with her at the latter end of 2005, when she was 32 and her Age Point had moved into Gemini in the 6th house. It was on the Balance Point, was soon to make a fact-gathering semi-sextile aspect to Saturn, and had already offered a challenging square to the Sun, both of them Pandora's Box pinning planets. When the Age Point is in the 6th house, the psychological drive is to establish oneself in the workplace and focus on the development of career. Imogen was having therapeutic lessons from an Alexander teacher and felt the need to learn as much as she could from this experience as she had already decided that she wanted to train and become a teacher herself. At that time she had said that she was seeking, searching and opening up to the new things she was learning from the Alexander Technique, and had also wanted to do some writing. I asked if with hindsight, in 2013, there had been any updates on this. She replied, "With hindsight Alexander Technique (AT) has offered everything that I wanted in terms of seeking, searching and opening up. Interestingly my professional development course is meaning that I am studying in very great depth the structure and organisation of writing & argument. In a lot of ways the AT work has taken the scales from my eyes so that I can just see what is there without twisting it according to my own preconceptions."

Age Points in Pandora's Box

Given that the Age Point either directly or indirectly contacts all the pinning planets in the Pandora's Box, I have mainly focussed on these and the conjunctions and oppositions made to date. Imogen was 11 when the Age Point made first contact with Jupiter in Aquarius, placed in the mutable zone of the 2nd house. With possible expressions of Jupiter in Aquarius in mind, I asked if she could recall any significant new experiences at this time, perhaps accompanied by a heightened sense of freedom. Was something interesting opening up for her? Maybe she began to realise that there was a vast amount of knowledge to be had "out there"? She said that starting senior school at this time brought a broadening of her mind and horizons. She particularly enjoyed science; it's an interest which has been retained along with skills that have been developed. When her Age Point was opposite Uranus at age 19, Imogen parted company with what she calls "hard physics" and started computer programming. She discovered that she was good at this and it currently underpins the 2nd house financial security of her full time job.

When Imogen was between the ages of 12 and 18, the Age Point was moving through the 3rd house. Moving through a large house such as this, experiences have less time to take root because there is a greater distance to be covered between the cusps. The duration and intensity of experiences are less than those in a smaller house, where life can seem hectic. However, there was a significant experience for Imogen when the Age Point was opposite her Leo Sun at age 13. Her Sun is high up in the chart, in the 9th house of higher learning and study. The Sun is not part of Pandora's Box but it aspects planets which form this pattern. It is involved in several other quadrangular aspect patterns which, like Pandora's Box, have a fixed quality and are motivated towards maintaining security and stability. The Sun gives the sense of self we gain through the use of the mind and will. In addition to this it represents, using the Huber Family Model technique, the father figure in our lives, and in the chart it gives clues about the person's relationship with their father. I asked Imogen if there were any experiences specifically connected with her father around this time. I also wondered if she began to gain a stronger sense of herself – did she become more determined, more able to make decisions and did she come into her own in some way? She agreed. "It was a time when dad and I were getting on particularly well" adding that she discovered they shared a sense of humour. "It was about this time, too, that I was beginning to get really interested in history. It was also when I was starting to find things that I really wanted to read. I'd probably date my love of history, books and reading to this period." Times were good and interesting too, as her new love of history took off. She describes how she was permanently buried in books. She still is; I've visited her home and seen walls lined with books, and piles of books on the floor awaiting attention.

The Venus/Pluto conjunction in Libra in the 9th house is strongly aspected and visually looks like a focal point in Imogen's chart. It suggests an intensity and charisma that she may not always be aware of, and an innate power which may be picked up by those she relates to. Imogen became aware of this at age 17, when her Age Point was opposite this conjunction, saying, "I definitely felt at this point that I no longer had to apologise for myself – that I was interested in things that other people I knew were not. I realised that I did not mind and that I would just follow the things that I liked." She speaks of not needing to feel she fitted in as she developed a sense of being her own person. She had entered the 6th form at school, and felt freer and able to follow her own direction. She also went through imagining various diverse career paths she could take, her choice reflecting the complexity and multiple possibilities in her chart.

The Age Point was conjunct strongly aspected Mars in the stress area before the 5th cusp in 1997, when Imogen was almost 24. Mars is not strongly placed at 4 degrees in Taurus, so Imogen is likely to experience pressure when there's a deadline to reach because of its stressed position before a cusp. Being well-aspected, Mars can draw upon the energies of the other 5 planets involved in the Pandora's Box. This may be draining, but Mars in Taurus offers a dogged determination to complete any task in hand. It has not been easy for Imogen to complete her Alexander training whilst doing a full-time job, and the determination will have kicked in here. Likewise, when she was at university working on her PhD, this determination also surfaced. She says, "The PhD started in 1994 but it was probably about 1995 that I started to knuckle down to it (here the Age Point had just passed the Low Point and was about to move into earthy, practical Taurus), and 1997 would be about the end of the PhD. This was a difficult time of trying to finish writing up but also having no money."

Age 36 brings with it a broadening view of life in general when the Age Point crosses the DC and enters the conscious, upper hemisphere of the chart. Imogen was psychologically prepared for this after her Age Point had been through the 6th house Low Point and she began to look ahead, planning long term for a change in career and life orientation. In 2008, with the Age Point moving through the mutable zone of the 6th house, she started her Alexander Technique training. Soon after it crossed the DC it was conjunct her Moon which symbolises the sense of self we gain through our feelings and emotions, along with how we connect with life in a child-like, open and sometimes fun-loving way. Imogen says, "I found myself on that course and felt it was a golden time for me. My life was fun and full of promise at this point and I felt lucky to be there and among a very special group of people. It was also at this point that I was beginning to see just how powerful the Alexander Technique was." This Age Point conjunction with the Moon activated the Small Talent triangle. It sits separately and to one side of the overall fixed quadrangular complex mass of aspect patterns, and has its own simplicity. With its flexible, mutable motivation, it is composed entirely of blue aspects and depends on the engagement of the individual to activate it and explore its potential. It's the aspect figure which is outside the box. Engaging with it offers Imogen a clarity and focus as it can point the way ahead for her in terms of developing her healing skills, her career and doing something she truly loves.

Imogen's Age Point is currently on the Low Point of the 7th house. At age 40, which coincides with this Low Point, a new life phase can begin. The Hubers say, "At this seventh house crisis point, we take account of ourselves and often adopt new goals and a healthier life style." With the Age Point conjunct Saturn ahead of her, Imogen's professional career development as an Alexander teacher will be unfolding; this conjunction will coincide with her taking on apprentice students of the Alexander Technique and being their tutor. Saturn, at its highest level, is the wise teacher whose motivation is to mentor and guide others.

* * * * *

Part 7

Summary and Conclusion

What to consider when using Age Progression

When I started writing this book, I noted the time and date of the event, set up the chart and then promptly forgot all about it. Curiosity sent me back to my database of charts as I neared this concluding section and, interested by what I saw, I decided to use the chart in this summary to illustrate the main points to consider in Age Progression. These are presented as bullet points for easy reference to help those readers who plan to use the techniques described in this book in a practical way with their own chart. Remember you'll need an accurate time of birth to ensure the greatest accuracy, and your chart should be set up using Koch Houses and with Huber style orbs and aspects.

Chart for the Creation of this Book

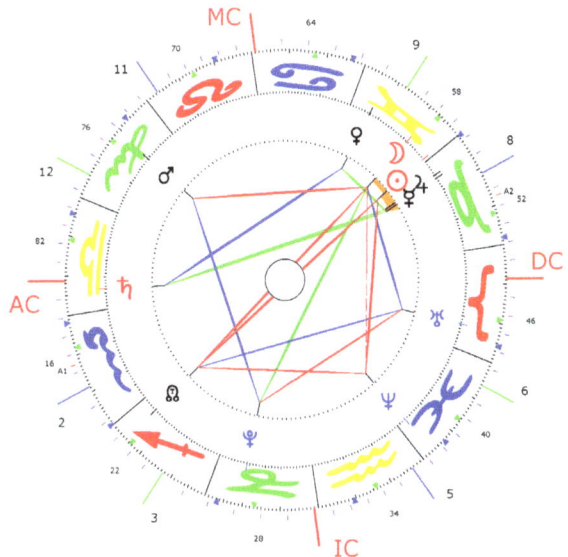

21.5.2012, 17:15, Knutsford, England

Age Point in the Houses

Things to consider:

- Which house is the Age Point currently in?
- Which life phase or area of life experience is being activated?
- Is the Age Point moving into a new house?

It has taken just over one year for me to write this book so the Age Point is in the 1st house. This is a significant, personal house where, in the chart of a person, individuality is laid down as the "I", or sense of self, is awakened and eventually formed as the Age Point progresses through this psychological life phase. The Age Point will take 6 years to travel through this and every subsequent house in the chart. After spending 6 years in a house, it moves into the next house where the theme of the new house will be uppermost. There is a looking forward and an engagement with matters associated with the next house after the Age Point has been through the Low Point.

Position of Age Point in the House

Things to consider:

- Where is the Age Point in the house?
- Is it in the cardinal, fixed or mutable zone?
- Is it on the Balance Point or Low Point of the house?
- Is it approaching the cusp and in the stress area?

As I write this, the book has recently had its first birthday and the Age Point is in the cardinal zone of the 1st house. When the Age Point is in the cardinal zone there is a lot of active, go ahead energy available to the individual, regardless of which house is involved. It is the house zone where tasks can be undertaken and completed as the energy is there to help move things along. The Balance Point is up ahead; the Age Point will reach it in just over a year. In the chart of a person, this would indicate a time when the demands of the environment are equally balanced with the output of energy available to the individual concerned. Everything can feel as if it's going fairly smoothly, and there could be a sense of busyness, of plenty happening.

Size of House
Things to consider:
- Is the house large or small?
- Is the house empty, or are there planets there?

The 1st house we're looking at is neither large nor small. It's roughly 26 degrees in size, as are most of the houses in this chart. That means the Age Point will not seem to move quickly (as in a large house) or slowly (as in a small house) but will move at a steady pace. It's not an empty house either as Saturn is in the cardinal zone, definitely indicating that there is work to be done! When the Age Point enters a house where there is a planet or planets, it's rather like entering a room with people in it. We can engage with the energy and quality of the planet or planets, but if we ignore them, we do so at our peril. They will return and demand attention in other guises via the subsequent aspects the Age Point makes to them as it travels around the chart.

Age Point and the Zodiac Signs
Things to consider:
- Which zodiac sign is the Age Point in?
- What is the sign's element - Fire, Earth, Air, Water?
- Does the sign have a cardinal, fixed or mutable quality?
- What kind of backdrop does this provide as the Age Point travels through?

In the book's chart the Age Point is in its rising sign of Libra, an air sign, and appropriate for a book which is concerned with communication and the sharing of ideas. Libran energy is focussed on representing fairness and is often linked with the qualities of beauty, balance, harmony and sometimes indecision. A cardinal sign, it's not known for holding back either, and when something requires attention it can be like an iron fist in a velvet glove as the cardinal energy is able to blend with the pleasant, equable drive of Libra. As a general backdrop for an individual, the Age Point moving through Libra will provide a flavour of easy communication and diplomacy.

Changing signs

Things to consider:

- Is the Age Point about to change signs, or has it already changed signs?

A change of sign by the Age Point is significant, as not only does the sign change, but the element does too. The book's Age Point moves on from Libra to Scorpio in its third year when the element will change from pleasant airy communication to watery intense depths when it enters Scorpio. Changes from fire to earth signs signal a move from enthusiastic activity to a more practical down to earth approach. When the Age Point moves from an earth to an air sign, the focus is on communication, learning and the sharing of ideas. A move from air to water will include more awareness of emotional matters and when the Age Point shifts from water to fire again there will be renewed energy, imbued with the qualities of the fire sign involved.

Age Point on one of the four cardinal points

Things to consider:

- Is the Age Point near the IC, where independence/individuality are asserted?
- Is the Age Point about to cross the DC? Is a coming into consciousness indicated?
- Is it on the MC, the highest point of the chart?
- Will the Age Point be going over the AC again, and what does this suggest?

The Age Point transit of all four cardinal points of the chart is significant and should always be considered carefully. At these points, which are high energy peaks, it also moves into a new quadrant of the chart so there are subtle changes in motivation and the orientation of inner energies taking place.

At age 18, when the Age Point crosses the IC, the individual wants to assert their independence and individuality, and not be tied so tightly by the expectations of upbringing. For many young people this time coincides closely with leaving home and the comfort of the nest, and striking out on their own. In terms of the book's Age Point, it has quite a way to go before this point is reached!

When the Age Point is on or near the DC at age 36, there can be a sense of personal awakening and a realisation that there is more "out there" and more to come than was ever previously realised. New horizons open up and beckon; the individual may feel at this time that the world is their oyster.

At age 54, the Age point is on the MC at the highest point of the chart. Here, the person often reaches their own professional peak, and can speak with authority from their own experience.

At age 72, the Age Point once again reaches the AC, beginning a second round of the chart as it moves back into the 1st house. This can be a liberating time, as the person will bring a lifetime of experience with them which can be shared with other, younger generations. As life expectancy is now greater than it was 50 years ago, it is significant that many more people will cross the AC and reach this second round of the chart – something to consider if the reader intends to work as a consultant using astrological psychology.

Aspects to the Planets

Things to consider:

- Is the Age Point conjunct or opposite a planet? These aspects have the greatest impact.
- Is it making other aspects to planets?
- What are the planets involved and what are their qualities?

As I've been writing this book, its Age Point has been conjunct 1st house Saturn for a lot of the time, and the Saturnian influence of getting on with the task in hand in a structured and disciplined way has definitely been in evidence. Interestingly this has been echoed in my own chart as my Age Point has also been conjunct Saturn while I've been writing (a coincidence or not?). The drive to write the book and share my experience of using Age Progression as a teacher and mentor has underpinned the project, and right now, as the conclusion and summary is reached, the Age Point in the book's chart has moved on to make a green quincunx aspect to the Mercury/Jupiter conjunction in Taurus.

Without a doubt, the conjunction and opposition aspects made by the Age Point are the strongest, but the green quincunx can also be very powerful as it brings deep learning experiences and suggests tenacity in reaching a desired goal. The planets aspected by the chart's quincunx are concerned with learning by information and fact-gathering (Mercury) and by widening perceptions and experience (Jupiter). I couldn't have planned this better if I'd tried!

In addition to the conjunction and opposition, other aspects made by the Age Point should also be considered, along with the colour of the aspect concerned, which offers information on the nature of the connection, plus the quality of the planet which is being aspected. This defines the nature and flavour of the experience.

Other points to note

Things to consider:

- Is the Age Point moving through an open space?
- Is the Age Point at the midpoint between two planets?

Sometimes the Age Point will be moving through an open empty space in the overall aspect structure. It might look as if nothing is going on, but something is almost always "going on" using Age Progression. If all the techniques introduced in this book are applied, such as position of the Age Point in the Dynamic Energy Curve in the houses, there will be plenty to work with. The Age Point in the book's chart appears to be entering an empty space as it moves away from its conjunction with Saturn en route to the Moon's Node. But if we take into account its movement through the signs, we see it's due to change fairly soon from airy Libra to watery intense Scorpio. The Age Point's movement through this 1st house will take it to the Balance Point at roughly the same time as this sign change takes place. It will continue to make aspects to all the other planets as it moves through the 1st house, and there will be a turning point and a change in orientation when the Age Point reaches the midpoint between Saturn and the Moon's Node.

Conclusion

At the start of this book I said that Age Progression and the movement of the Age Point can be used for personal development and greater self-understanding when working on your own chart. As it's not static it can be a very useful resource to draw upon whenever we hit a rough patch in life or are not sure about which direction to take. Without a doubt, it offers a wealth of insights into what is being experienced at a given time and how this might manifest.

We can use Age Progression to look back on our life and review where we've come from and it can be used to help identify past behaviours and responses to situations in earlier life phases. It can also show us that things will move on and can encourage us not to feel stuck in any one place or situation indefinitely, unless we choose this. Age Progression can be used effectively as a personal tool, as well as with clients by professional astrologers and counsellors trained in the Huber Method of astrological psychology. Now it's over to you, the reader, to try out this impressive tool for yourself. May it offer you many valuable insights.

Resources

Astrological Psychology Association

A MODERN APPROACH to SELF-AWARENESS and PERSONAL GROWTH

Astrology is now recognised as providing a valuable tool for the development of self awareness and human potential. Bruno and Louise Huber researched and developed astrological psychology over many years, combining the best of astrology with Roberto Assagioli's psychosynthesis.

DIPLOMA IN ASTROLOGICAL PSYCHOLOGY
 Learn astrological psychology
 Understand yourself and help others

FOUNDATION COURSES IN ASTROLOGY
 The basics of astrology

MEMBERSHIP
 Community of interest, magazine, discounts...

ONLINE RESOURCES
 Prospectus, bookshop, consultants, forum...

www.astrologicalpsychology.org

Enquiries: enquiries@astrologicalpsychology.org

Teaching Astrological Psychology since 1983

APA Bookshop

Books and APA publications related to the Huber Method.
Linda Tinsley, APA Bookshop
70 Kensington Road, Southport PR9 0RY, UK
Tel: 00 44 (0)1704 544652, Email: lucindatinsley@tiscali.co.uk

Huber Chart Data Service

Provides colour-printed Huber-style charts and chart data.
Richard Llewellyn, Huber Chart Data Service
PO Box 29, Upton, Wirral CH49 3BG, UK
Tel: 00 44 (0)151 606 8551, Email: r.llewellyn@btinternet.com

Software for Huber-style Charts

AstroCora, MegaStar, Regulus

On CD: Elly Gibbs Tel: 00 44 (0)151-677-0779
          Email: software.huber@btinternet.com
Download: Cathar Software Website: www.catharsoftware.com

Selected Publications on Astrological Psychology

The Cosmic Egg Timer
by Joyce Hopewell & Richard Llewellyn

Introduces astrological psychology. Use your own birth chart alongside this book and gain insights into the kind of person you are, what makes you tick, and which areas of life offer you the greatest potential.

Aspect Pattern Astrology

Understanding motivation through aspect patterns. Essential reference work. The aspect pattern reveals the structure and basic motivations of our consciousness. Over 45 distinct aspect figures are identified, each with its own meaning.

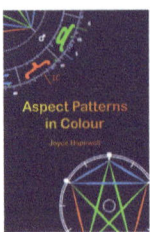

Aspect Patterns in Colour
by Joyce Hopewell

Features all the main aspect patterns, fully indexed and illustrated in colour, with the meaning of each figure, example charts and interpretations. A valuable reference.

Astrological Psychosynthesis

Astrology as a Pathway to Growth. Bruno Huber's introduction to this holistic approach to astrology and Assagioli's psychosynthesis, following the premise that the soul is at the root of all developmental processes. Focus on intelligence, integration, relationships.

Moon Node Astrology

Combines psychological understanding with the concept of reincarnation, bringing a new astrological focus on the shadow personality and the individual's evolutionary process. Includes the psychological approach used with the Moon's Nodes and the Node Chart.

* *Books by Bruno & Louise Huber except where authors otherwise indicated.*

A Modern Approach to Self Awareness and Personal Growth

The Living Birth Chart
by Joyce Hopewell

Aims to provide insight into the full power of the Huber Method and give a feel for its practical use, with numerous examples and exercises enabling the reader to experience the approach for themselves.

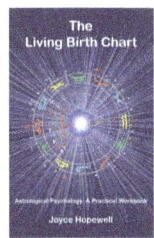

The Planets and their Psychological Meaning

Shows how the positions of the planets are fundamental to horoscope interpretation. They represent basic archetypal qualities present in everyone, giving clues to psychological abilities and characteristics, growth and spiritual development.

LifeClock

The horoscope is seen as a clock for the person's lifetime, with the Age Point indicating their age as the 'time' on the clock. Those trying it invariably find significant correspondences between indications in their birth chart and meaningful events in their lives.

The Astrological Houses

The psychological significance of the houses is explained and the intensity curve shows how positioning within a house affects energy flow, introducing Low Points, Stress Planets, the effect on Age Progression etc.

Transformation

Astrology as a Spiritual Path. Describes processes of transformation and personal/spiritual growth as natural stages in human development, related to astrological indicators in the birth chart. New material on Dynamic Houses, Stress Planets, House Chart, Integration Chart.

Published by HopeWell: www.hopewellpublisher.com

www.ingramcontent.com/pod-product-compliance
Lightning Source LLC
Chambersburg PA
CBHW072148160426
43197CB00012B/2297